Bryn Mawr Latin Commentaries

Plautus Mercator

Antonios C. Augoustakis

Thomas Library
Bryn Mawr College
Bryn Mawr, Pennsylvania

The Bryn Mawr Latin Commentaries have been supported by a generous
grant from the Division of Education Programs of the
National Endowment for the Humanities

Copyright 2009 by Bryn Mawr Commentaries

Manufactured in the United States of America
ISBN (10) 1-931019-06-1
(13) 9781931019064

Printed by
Bryn Mawr Commentaries
Thomas Library
Bryn Mawr College
Bryn Mawr PA 19010

Bryn Mawr Latin Commentaries

Editors

Julia Haig Gaisser   James J. O'Donnell

Bryn Mawr College   *Georgetown University*

The purpose of the Bryn Mawr Latin Commentaries is to make a wide range of classical and post-classical authors accessible to the intermediate student. Each commentary provides the minimum grammatical and lexical information necessary for a first reading of the text.

Acknowledgments

My journey in Plautus began in the 1990s when I was an undergraduate at the University of Crete. I was attracted to the *Mercator* in particular in the Spring semester of 2003, when I taught the play to a group of students in Rome, during the Baylor in Italy summer program in July. The quality and size of the play, as well as the lack of a commentary in English, led to me to undertake the project. That same summer, on a warm afternoon the students gave a wonderful performance of the play at the Anfiteatro Quercia del Tasso on the Janicolo, both in Latin and in English.

First and foremost, I would like to express my gratitude to the editor, Julia Haig Gaisser. Julia read and corrected several drafts of this commentary; without her criticism and meticulousness, I could not have completed this volume. Rick Hamilton patiently and bravely formatted the commentary and made the final changes proposed, for which I remain in his debt. I am grateful to several students for their comments throughout this process, especially Erik Ellis, Heather Outland, Faith Wardlaw, and Becky West. They read drafts of the commentary and offered corrections and suggestions on how to make this edition more useful to an undergraduate audience. To all the students in my Plautus seminars I dedicate then this edition.

Introduction

A. Plautus and Roman Comedy

We have little certain information about the playwright called Titus Maccius Plautus. In all probability he was born around 254 and died in 184 BCE. Sarsinna, a city in Umbria, has traditionally been considered his birthplace. He purportedly started his career there, perhaps as both an actor and a playwright. His *cognomen*, Plautus, probably refers to a physical defect, as it means "flat-footed" or "flat-eared," an adjective also often used for mime-actors. His *nomen*, Maccius, is associated with a stock character, a clown, in Italian farces. His *praenomen*, Titus, refers to his father, but it also means "penis" and alludes to the phallus used in farce and mime performances. Our author's full name, therefore ("Phallus son of Clown, the Mime actor"), is nothing other than a combination of three nicknames derived from his career. Plautus wrote many comedies, of which twenty-one survive (some in only fragmentary condition).

Roman comedy owes many of its themes and characters to Greek New Comedy (ca. 330-250). The plays of Greek New Comedy were inspired by themes of everyday life like the vicissitudes of young lovers, the reunions of long-lost children with their parents, the generational gap between the old and young. They featured stock characters (clever slaves, angry or indulgent fathers, foolish young men, shrewish wives, innocent and not so innocent young women, and the like); and they were performed in five acts, separated by musical interludes that filled in the time for scene and costume changes. There were several authors of New Comedy. Among those particularly important for Plautus are Menander (ca. 344-292/1) and Philemon (ca. 361-263/2).

New Comedy became very popular in Southern Italy and Sicily after around 290. The Greek plays found a ready audience in these largely Greek-speaking regions, and soon the genre was combined with native Italian forms of entertainment like Atellan farce and mime. Atellan farce was a kind of unscripted burlesque comedy featuring stock characters with masks, such as the fool, the grandfather, the clown (Bucco, Pappus, Maccus). In mimes unmasked characters staged and ridiculed stock situations (adultery was a favorite). The combination of New Comedy with mime and Atellan farce produced a new Italian genre, the Roman *fabula palliata* (literally "Latin play wearing a Greek cloak"), which reached its apogee with Plautus and Terence. The Latin comedies all take place in Greece. Most often they have their inspiration from original plays of Greek New Comedy, which the Roman poets transferred into Latin verse and meter. In the case of the *Mercator*, as Plautus says in the Prologue, the theme and plot are borrowed from the homonymous play by Philemon (Ἔμπορος = *Merchant*). (There is also a Greek comedy with the same title by Diphilus.) The *Mercator*, like Plautus' other plays, features an interchange of dialogue, recitative (lively discussion or soliloquy with musical accompaniment), and songs, the so-called *cantica*. The date of the play is uncertain. Scholars have proposed dates ranging from 211-210 to 190-188 BCE.

Further Reading

1. On New Comedy and Plautus

Christenson, D. (ed. and com.) 2000. Plautus *Amphitruo*. Cambridge.
Gratwick, A. S. (ed. and com.) 1993. Plautus *Menaechmi*. Cambridge.
———. 1973. "'Titus Maccius Plautus.'" *Classical Quarterly* 23: 78-84.
Hunter, R. L. 1985. *The New Comedy of Greece and Rome*. Cambridge.
Lefèvre, E. 1995. *Plautus und Philemon*. Tübingen.
The fragments of Philemon can be found in: R. Kassel - C. Austin (eds.) 1989. *Poetae Comici Graeci*, vol. VII. Berlin.

2. On Plautine Comedy

Anderson, W. S. 1993. *Barbarian Play. Plautus' Roman Comedy*. Toronto.
Buck, C. H. Jr. 1940. *A Chronology of the Plays of Plautus*. Baltimore.
Fraenkel, E. 2007. *Plautine Elements in Plautus*. Oxford (English Translation of the 1922 German monograph).
Konstan, D. 1983. *Roman Comedy*. Ithaca.
Leigh, M. 2004. *Comedy and the Rise of Rome*. Oxford: 98-157.
McCarthy, K. 2000. *Slaves, Masters and the Art of Authority in Plautine Comedy*. Princeton.

Marshall, C. W. 2006. *The Stagecraft and Performance of Roman Comedy*. Cambridge.
Moore, T. J. 1998. *The Theater of Plautus. Playing to the Audience*. Austin.
Schutter, K. H. E. 1952. *Quibus Annis Comoediae Plautinae Primum Actae Sint Quaeritur*. Groningen.
Segal, E. 1968. *Roman Laughter. The Comedy of Plautus*. Cambridge, Mass.
Slater, N. 1985. *Plautus in Performance: The Theatre of the Mind*. Princeton.

B. Language of Plautus

Archaic Latin is one of the features that make Plautus' plays special. The following are some notable differences between archaic and classical Latin:

1. Nouns
a. Nouns of the first declension use the alternative bisyllabic genitive ending *–āī* for the diphthong *–ae* (e.g., *familiai*).
b. Nouns, adjectives, and pronouns of the second declension have *–ŏ-* (the Greek ending for second declension nouns) in the nominative singular masculine instead of *–ŭ-* after a consonantal *–u-* (e.g., *seruos*); in the plural, nouns often end in *–ei* instead of *–ī* (e.g., *seruei= serui*).
c. Archaic vocatives, such as *puere* ("boy"), are frequent.
d. Some nouns of the third declension end in *–os* for *–or* (e.g., *labos*); nouns of the third declension with an *i*-stem are most often found with an *i-* instead of an *e-* ending (e.g., *nauim= nauem*).

2. Verbs
a. The stem *uŏ -* is used for the classical *uĕ -* (e.g., *aduorto, reuorti*).
b. Frequentative forms are preferred (e.g., *dicito, parito*).
c. Passive infinitives end in *–ier*, instead of an *–i* (e.g., *amarier, adgredier*).
d. Future imperatives in *–to* for the second and third person singular, although rare in classical Latin, are used when the command has a precise reference to future time (e.g., *facito, dicito*).

e. Characteristic is the lack of syncopation in *uolo, nolo, malo* (e.g., *mauelim= malim, neuis= non uis*), whereas the contracted form of *si uis* appears as *sis*, "please, if you wish."
f. Archaic subjunctives of *sum* are common (e.g., *siem, sies, siet*); the subjunctive *fuat= sit* is formed from the stem of the perfect tense.
g. The archaic future (or future perfect) of *facio* is *faxo*; also frequent are the perfect subjunctives of verbs such as *facio* and *audeo*, in the forms *faxint= fecerint* and *ausim= ausus sim*. These were originally aorist optatives (Lindsay, *Syntax* II.24).
h. The verb *do* presents a variety of archaic present indicative and subjunctive forms (e.g., *danunt= dant*; *duit= det*; *duas= dederis*).
i. Syncopated forms of perfect or pluperfect are preferred (e.g., *inlexe= inlexisse*; *obduxe= obduxisse*; *recesset= recessisset*; *parasse= parauisse*).
j. The lengthened stem *ei-* for *ī-* is common (e.g., *deicere*; *deixis= dixeris*).
k. The future of fourth conjugation verbs is formed not in *–iam* but in *–ibo*, as in the first and second conjugations (e.g., *seruibo= seruiam*).

3. Adjectives, Pronouns, Prepositions

a. Superlative adjectives end in *–umus* (*-uma, -umum*) for *–imus* (e.g., *proxumus*).
b. *quom* is used for *cum* (see nouns 1b above); notice that the combination *quo-* replaces *cu-* in such instances as *quoi, quom*.
c. the suffix *–c(e)* is frequently added to pronouns such as *hic* or *ille* for emphasis (e.g., *huiusce, illic*); other common suffixes are: *-pte, -te, -met*. Cf. also *med* for *me* to avoid hiatus.
d. *ecce* is combined with demonstrative, relative, interrogative, and indefinite pronouns into one word, such as *eccillum* or *eccum*; *ecquam*; *equisnam*.
e. *ipsus* is used instead of *ipse*.
f. The following prefixes are preferred: *aps-* and *op-* for *ab-* and *ob-* (e.g., *apsterge, opsequar*).
g. The interrogative particle *–ne* appears almost always elided as *–n* at the end of words, after crasis with the final *–s* of the previous word (e.g., *uiden, uin, satin, potine*).
h. *qui* is used for *quo* as an adverbial ablative ("how, whereby").

Further Reading
Bennett, C. E. 1910-1914. *Syntax of Early Latin*. 2 vols. Boston [reprint Hildesheim 1966].
Hammond, M., Mack, A. M., Moskalew, W. (ed. and com.) 1963. *T. Macci Plauti* Miles Gloriosus. Cambridge, Mass: 49-57.
Lindsay, W. M. 1907. *The Syntax of Plautus*. Oxford.
de Melo, W. D. C. 2007. *The Early Latin Verb System: Archaic Forms in Plautus, Terence, and Beyond*. Oxford.

C. Meter

a. Prosody
1. <u>Syllabification</u>: Quantitative meter is based on various patterns of long and short syllables. The number of syllables in each word depends on the number of vowels and diphthongs (two vowels pronounced as one, such as *ae, au, ei, oe,* or *ui*). Words are divided into syllables according to the following rules:
    a. If a vowel or diphthong is followed by a single consonant, that consonant is taken with the next syllable. The first syllable ends with a short or long vowel and is called *open* (e.g., *sa-pi-o* has three open syllables).
    b. If the vowel or diphthong is followed by two or more consonants, division takes place between the consonants, with the first consonant closing the previous syllable (*closed syllables* are always long), while the second begins a new syllable (e.g., in *con-ten-ta* the first two syllables are closed, the last one is open). The same rules apply at the end of a word (e.g., in *ad-uo-la-ui-t in-uo-co* the fourth syllable *–ui* is left open). Notice that x (= cs) and z (= ds) count as two consonants, but the combination *qu* as one, whereas *h,* even in combination (*ch, th, ph*), is considered only an aspiration, not a consonant.
    In early Latin, however, if the first consonant is a mute (*b, p, d, t, g,* or *c*) and the second consonant is a liquid (*l* or *r*), the two consonants are never separated but rather leave the preceding syllable open (e.g., *ma-tru-mo-ni-o*). Notice also that in the beginning of a new word, two consonants (mute and liquid or *st, sc*) do not necessarily affect the quantity of the final vowel of the preceding word.

Also, in early Latin, the final consonants *–s* and *–m* are weakly pronounced and do not automatically close the final syllable of a word. In this edition, the weak final *–s* is marked as elided by the use of an apostrophe (e.g., *Venu'*, 38).

2. Elision, Prodelision: If a word ending with a vowel or *-m* is followed by a word beginning with a vowel, diphthong, or **h**, the first of the adjacent syllables is suppressed, in what is called *elision* (e.g., *cur-ren-dum et= cur-ren-d(um) et*). If the second word is a form of *sum* starting with a vowel (e.g., *est* or *es*), the process (*prodelision*) is reversed (e.g., *opust= opus est*, 1004). Prodelision of *es* in this edition is marked by an apostrophe after nouns, adjectives, or participles to avoid possible confusion with other forms (e.g., *redempta's*, 529; *sana's*, 682).

Often, however, elision is omitted, leaving a "gap" or *hiatus* between the two words (e.g. *credo humanas*, 6), which is marked in this text by a vertical line | between the words. Hiatus occurrs frequently at the *caesura* or *diaeresis* of the iambic senarii and the trochaic (and iambic) septenarii or at a pause or change of speaker.

3. Word Accent: The natural Latin word accent plays a significant role in early Latin scansion. A monosyllabic word is usually unaccented, while bisyllabic words are accented on the penultimate syllable, since no word is accented on its ultimate syllable (but note that apocopated words, such as *illíc*, receive an accent on the ultimate, because of the dropping of the final *–e*). For polysyllabic words, the following rule applies: in words of three syllables, the antepenultimate is accented if the penultimate is short; in words of more than three syllables, the first syllable is accented, but if the penultimate is long, it may receive a second accent. The laws of accent apply also to groups of words, i.e., expressions, such as *operám dare*. The enclitics (*-que*, *-ue*, *-ne*, *-ce*) also affect the accent's place.

4. Quantity of Syllables: A syllable is long if it contains a long vowel or diphthong (*long by nature*) or if it is closed (*long by position*).

a. In archaic Latin, some final syllables preserve their original long quantity, whereas in classical Latin they are scanned as short. The endings *–at, -et, -it* are usually long, except for the futures in *–bit*, the future perfect, and the present and future indicative of the third conjugation (and the third conjugation *–io* verbs). The endings *-ar*, *-er*, *-or*, and *–al* also count as long.

b. A common feature of Plautine scansion is *iambic shortening* (also called the law of *breuis breuians*): a long syllable is shortened if it is preceded by a short syllable *and* the word accent falls on the syllable immediately preceding or following. Words like ĕgō, īllĕ, or bĕnē are frequently subject to iambic shortening, but word groups are also subject to it. E.g.:

⏑ ⏑ –

ad uxórem, 244

[*ux-*, long by nature, counts as short because it is preceded by the short syllable *ad* and followed by an accented syllable.]

c. Sometimes two contiguous vowels in adjacent syllables (i.e., not a diphthong) may be treated as a single long syllable (*synizesis*). In Plautus this is common in forms of *meus, tuus, suus, is, idem, deus*; in *huius, illius, quoius* (= *cuius*), perfect forms of *sum* (e.g., *fuisse*, 470), *rei, dies*.

d. Often a monosyllabic word with a long vowel, a diphthong, or short vowel + *–m* is shortened before a short vowel, instead of being elided, in what is called *prosodic hiatus* (e.g. rĕm ăgī, 1010).

b. Metrical Patterns

The most frequently used metrical patterns in Plautus are the iambic (⏑ –) and the trochaic (– ⏑).

Iamb	⏑ –
Trochee	– ⏑
Anapest	⏑ ⏑ –
Dactyl	– ⏑ ⏑
Spondee	– –
Pyrrhic	⏑ ⏑
Tribrach	⏑ ⏑ ⏑
Proceleusmatic	⏑ ⏑ ⏑ ⏑
Choriamb	– ⏑ ⏑ –
Bacchic	⏑ – –
Molossus	– – –
Cretic	– ⏑ –
Ionic a minore	⏑ ⏑ – –

Ionic a maiore   – – ᴗ ᴗ
First Paeon   – ᴗ ᴗ ᴗ
Fourth Paeon   ᴗ ᴗ ᴗ –

    Since a long syllable is regarded as the equivalent of two shorts, substitutions are allowed in some meters. In some cases allowable substitutions are not necessarily "equivalent"; e.g., an iamb [ᴗ –] may be replaced by a spondee, dactyl, anapest, tribrach, or proceleusmatic. The last syllable in a verse may be either long or short (called *anceps* and marked by ×), but by convention is usually counted and marked as long.

    In spoken or sung verse iambs and trochees are measured in feet (thus a line of six iambs is called iambic senarius). Other rhythms are measured in *metra*, which may consist of one foot (cretics, bacchics) or two (anapests).

    In some meters word break occurs regularly at fixed points in the verse. Word division coinciding with a break between feet or metra is called a *diaeresis* (::); a division not coinciding with a metrical break between feet is called a *caesura* (//). Note that hiatus is allowed at the *caesura* or *diaeresis* of a verse. The line-segments between *caesurae* or *diaereseis* are called *cola* ("limbs"). The metrical accent (beat), *ictus*, always falls on the long element. There is preference for a pure iamb or a pure trochee as the last foot of the iambic and trochaic meters, but remember that the last element can often admit a *breuis in longo* (i.e., a short instead of a long syllable).

1. Iambic Meters
1. **Iambic Senarius** (six iambic feet, ᴗ –):
Substitutions are allowed in all but the sixth foot, which must be an iamb. The following substitutions are allowed: ᴗ ᴗ –, – –, ᴗ ᴗ ᴗ, – ᴗ ᴗ, ᴗ ᴗ ᴗ ᴗ. *Caesura* usually occurs after the fifth element (third foot) but sometimes is found after the third and seventh elements. If *diaeresis* occurs at the end of the second or fourth foot, that foot must be a pure iamb (Meyer's Law).

    – ᴗ ᴗ| – – | ᴗ ᴗ ᴗ ᴗ| ᴗ ᴗ ᴗ – | – | ᴗ ᴗ
    multiloquium :: parumlóqui(um) hoc // ideo fit quia (31)

[Note: *-rum* is short by iambic shortening.]

2. Iambic Septenarius (seven and a half iambic feet, ∪ −):
For the allowable substitutions for the iamb see on the Iambic Senarius. The end of the fourth foot coincides with a *diaeresis*, thus dividing the line in two halves. The fourth foot is generally an iamb; but if a *caesura* occurs in the fifth foot, the fourth foot takes the form × −.

```
 − − | ∪            − | − − | ∪ ∪ |   −         − | − − | ∪ − | −
```
n(am) illi quid(em) hau sane diust :: quom // dentes exciderunt (541)

3. Iambic Octonarius (eight iambic feet, ∪ −):
Caesura and *diaeresis* occurs as in the septenarius.

```
∪ − | − − | − −  | ∪ − |  ∪ ∪   − | ∪ − |  −  − | −
```
perii seditionem facit :: lien // óccupat praecordia (124)

[Note: *–en* in *lien* is short by iambic shortening.]

2. Trochaic Meters
1. Trochaic Septenarius (seven and a half feet, − ∪):
The following substitutions for the trochee are allowed: − −, − ∪ ∪, ∪ ∪ −, ∪ ∪ ∪, ∪ ∪ ∪ ∪. There is usually *diaeresis* after the fourth foot; if not, there is *diaeresis* after the fifth foot and *caesura* in the fourth.

```
∪ ∪   − | −       ∪ | − − | − −  |  −          − | − − | − − | − | −
```
mihi data (e)st hic emit illam :: pulchr(e) // os subleuit patri (604)

2. Trochaic Octonarius (eight feet, − ∪):
Diaeresis occurs as in the septenarius.

```
∪ ∪ − | − − | ∪ ∪ − | − − | ∪ ∪ − | − − | ∪ ∪  − | ∪ ∪
```
miser amicam mihi paraui :: animi caussa preti(o) eripui (341)

3. Lyric Meters
Meters in the *cantica* vary. Here are the lyric meters encountered in the *Mercator*:

1. Iambic Dimeter (two iambic metra, ∪ − ∪ −):
For the allowable substitutions see on the Iambic Senarius.

```
  ∪ −   ∪ − |−   ∪ ∪∪ −
```
quid est negoti? periimus (135)

9

2. **Bacchic Tetrameter** (four bacchic metra, ∪ - -):
The following substitutions are allowed: - - -, ∪ ∪ - -, - - ∪ ∪, - ∪ ∪ ∪,
∪ ∪ ∪ -, - ∪ ∪ -. There is a *diaeresis* after the second foot or a
caesura after the fifth or seventh elements.

- - -|- - -|- - -|∪ - -

is resciuit et uidit // et perdidit me (343)

3. **Anapestic Dimeter** (two anapestic metra, ∪ ∪ - ∪ ∪ -):
The following substitutions are allowed: - ∪ ∪, - -, ∪ ∪ ∪ ∪.

∪ ∪ ∪ ∪ | ∪ ∪ - |∪ ∪ - |∪ ∪ -

ita mihi mala res aliqu(a) obicitur (339)

Further Reading:
Halporn, J., Ostwald, M., Rosenmeyer, T. G. 1994. *The Meters of Greek and Latin Poetry*. Indianapolis.
Hammond, M., Mack, A. M., Moskalew, W. (ed. and comm.) 1963. *T. Macci Plauti Miles Gloriosus*. Cambridge, Mass: 49-57.
Lindsay, W. M. 1922. *Early Latin Verse*. Oxford.
Questa, C. 1967. *Introduzione alla Metrica di Plauto*. Bologna.
-------. 2007. *La Metrica di Plauto e di Terenzio*. Urbino.
Raven, D. 1965. *Latin Metre*. London.

D. Text and Variant Readings

This Latin text of the *Mercator* differs from that of W. M. Lindsay's Oxford Classical Text edition (1904) in the following places (Lindsay's reading is given after //):

Arg. I 5 *ac* // *at*
Arg. II 6 <*ait*>
17 †*meam perconatus rem inde exorsus sum ilico*† // †*per mea percontatus sum uos sumque inde exilico*†
26 *temeritas* // *temeritast*
29 *inertia* // *inerit etiam*
81 *odio me esse* // *odio* †*esse me*†
126 (transferred after 127)
129 †*ex hoc metu ut sim certus*† // *ex hoc metu ut sim certus*
153 *cis* // * (lacuna)
182 *rogo* // *interrogo*
220 *aspiciet* // *aspicit*
276 *atque illius hic nunc simiae* // *ac metuo ne illaec simiae*

partis ferat   // partis ferat
282 *ei // i*
282 *adicere // dicere*
309 *ac //* [*ac*]
312 *ut tu me amando   // ut med amando*
319 *peccare humanumst // humanum amarest*
320 *humanum amarest* (tranferred from 319) //
   <*humanum*> *** (lacuna)
338 *mi euenire quod cupio // mi quod cupio euenire*
371-372 (deleted)
458 *illi quoidam // illic quidam*
497 *melius sanus sis // meliust sanus sis*
511a (added)
571 *ausculari // osculari*
573 *amem // ames*
598a-b (deleted)
619-624 (deleted)
687a (added) // *** (lacuna)
689 *ei // i*
773 †*incommodi*† // *incommodi*
782 *sequimini // sequiminei*
830 *superum*<*que*> *// superum* (hiatus)
839 *ubi qui amici, qui infideles // ubique amici qui infideles*
   sint // sient
842 *spectatrix   // speratrix*
843 <*tibi*> (added)
849 *lacuna* after this verse
887 (tranferred after 872)
   †*sta ilico*†   // *sta ilico*
878 *nonne ex aduorso uides // huc ex aduorso uide sis*
879 *nubis atra imberque* <*ut*> *instat? // nubis ater imberque instat—*
   aspice ad sinisteram, // aspicin?—ad sinisteram.
880 *atque ut dei is*<*tuc uorti iubent*> // *nonne ex aduorso uides?*
895 *quin // qui*
920 *omnibus hic ludificatur me // omnibus me ludificatur hic*
970 *degeneres fiiunt //* †*genere capiunt*†
983a (deleted)
988 *hercle // hercl'*
996 *para clientem // para me clientem*

Plautus *Mercator*

ARGVMENTVM I

Missus mercatum | ab suo adulescens patre
Emit atque adportat scita forma mulierem.
Requirit quae sit, postquam eam uidit, senex:
Confingit seruos emptam matri pedisequam.
Amat senex hanc, ac se simulans uendere   5
Tradit uicino; | eum putat uxor sibi
Obduxe scortum. tum Charinum | ex fuga
Retrahit sodalis, postquam amicam | inuenit.

ARGVMENTVM II

Mercatum asotum filium extrudit pater.
is peregre missus redimit ancillam hospitis
amore captus, aduehit. naue exilit,
pater aduolat, uisam | ancillam deperit.
cuius sit percontatur; seruus pedisequam   5
ab adulescente matri <ait> emptam ipsius.
senex, sibi prospiciens, ut amico suo
ueniret natum orabat, natus ut suo·
hic filium subdiderat uicini, pater
uicinum; praemercatur ancillam senex.   10
eam domi deprehensam coniunx illius
uicini scortum insimulat, protelat uirum.
mercator expes patria fugere destinat,
prohibetur a sodale, qui patrem illius
orat cum patre suopte, nato ut cederet.   15

PERSONAE

CHARINVS ADVLESCENS	EVTYCHVS ADVLESCENS
ACANTHIO SERVVS	PASICOMPSA MERETRIX
DEMIPHO SENEX	DORIPPA MATRONA
LYSIMACHVS SENEX	SYRA ANVS
LORARIVS	COCVS

SCAENA ATHENIS

T. MACCI PLAVTI MERCATOR

ACTVS I

CHARINVS　　　　　　　　　　　　I.i

Duas res simul nunc agere decretumst mihi:
et argumentum et meos amores eloquar.
non ego item facio ut alios in comoediis
<ui> uidi amoris facere, qui aut Nocti aut Dii
aut Soli aut Lunae miserias narrant suas:　　　　5
quos pol ego credo | humanas querimonias
non tanti facere, quid uelint, quid non uelint;
uobis narrabo potius meas nunc miserias.
Graece haec uocatur Emporos Philemonis,　'
eadem Latine Mercator Macci Titi.　　　　　　10
pater ad mercatum hinc me meus misit Rhodum;
biennium iam factum est, postquam abii domo.
ibi amare occepi forma eximia mulierem.
sed ea ut sim implicitus dicam, si operaest auribus
atque aduortendum ad animum adest benignitas.　15
et hoc parum hercle more amatorum institi:
†meam perconatus rem inde exorsus sum ilico.†
nam amorem haec cuncta uitia sectari solent,
cura aegritudo nimiaque elegantia,
haec non modo illum qui amat, sed quemque attigit　20
magno atque solido multat infortunio,
nec pol profecto quisquam sine grandi malo
praequam res patitur studuit elegantiae.
sed amori accedunt etiam haec, quae dixi minus:
insomnia, aerumna, error, terror et fuga,　　　25
ineptia stultitiaque adeo et temeritas,
incogitantia excors, inmodestia,
petulantia et cupiditas, maliuolentia;
inertia, auiditas, desidia, iniuria,

inopia, contumelia et dispendium, 30
multiloquium, parumloquium: hoc ideo fit quia
quae nihil attingunt ad rem nec sunt usui,
tam amator profert saepe aduorso tempore;
hoc pauciloquium rusum idcirco praedico,
quia nullus umquam amator adeost callide 35
facundus, quae in rem sint suam ut possit loqui.
nunc uos mi irasci ob multiloquium non decet:
eodem quo amorem Venu' mi hoc legauit die.
illuc reuorti certumst, conata eloquar.
principio <ut ex> ephebis aetate exii 40
atque animus studio amotus pueril ist meus,
amare ualide coepi hinc meretricem: ilico
res exsulatum ad illam clam abibat patris.
leno inportunus, dominus eius mulieris,
ui summa ut quidque poterat rapiebat domum. 45
obiurigare pater haec noctes et dies,
perfidiam, iniustitiam lenonum expromere;
lacerari ualide suam rem, illius augerier.
summo haec clamore; interdum mussans conloqui:
abnuere, negitare adeo me natum suom. 50
conclamitare tota urbe et praedicere,
omnes tenerent mutuitanti credere.
amorem multos inlexe in dispendium:
intemperantem, non modestum, iniurium
trahere, exhaurire me quod quirem ab se domo; 55
ratione pessuma a me ea quae ipsus optuma
omnis labores inuenisset perferens,
in amoribus diffunditari ac didier.
conuicium tot me annos iam se pascere;
quod nisi puderet, ne luberet uiuere. 60
sese extemplo ex ephebis postquam excesserit,
non, ut ego, amori neque desidiae in otio
operam dedisse, neque potestatem sibi
fuisse; adeo arte cohibitum esse <se> a patre:
multo opere inmundo rustico se exercitum 65
neque nisi quinto anno quoque solitum uisere
urbem, atque extemplo inde, ut spectauisset peplum,
rus rusum confestim exigi solitum a patre.

ibi multo primum sese familiarium
laborauisse, quom haec pater sibi diceret: 70
"tibi aras, tibi occas, tibi seris, tibi idem metis,
tibi denique iste pariet laetitiam labos."
postquam recesset uita patrio corpore,
agrum se uendidisse atque ea pecunia
nauem, metretas quae trecentas tolleret, 75
parasse atque ea se mercis uectatum undique,
adeo dum, quae tum haberet, peperisset bona;
me idem decere, si ut deceret me forem.
ego me ubi inuisum meo patri esse intellego 79-80
atque odio me esse quoi placere aequom fuit,
amens amansque ui | animum offirmo meum,
dico esse iturum me mercatum, si uelit:
amorem missum facere me, dum illi opsequar.
agit gratias mi atque ingenium adlaudat meum; 85
sed mea promissa non neglexit persequi.
aedificat nauim cercurum et mercis emit,
parata naui imponit, praeterea mihi
talentum argenti ipsus sua adnumerat manu;
seruom una mittit, qui olim puero paruolo 90
mihi paedagogus fuerat, quasi uti mihi foret
custos. his sic confectis nauem soluimus.
Rhodum uenimus, ubi quas merces uexeram
omnis ut uolui uendidi ex sententia.
lucrum ingens facio praeterquam mihi meu' pater 95
dedit aestumatas merces: ita peculium
conficio grande. sed dum in portu illi ambulo,
hospes me quidam adgnouit, ad cenam uocat.
uenio, decumbo acceptus hilare atque ampliter.
discubitum noctu ut imus, ecce ad me aduenit 100
mulier, qua mulier alia nullast pulchrior;
ea nocte mecum illa hospitis iussu fuit.
uosmet uidete quam mihi ualde placuerit:
postridie hospitem adeo, oro ut uendat mihi,
dico eius pro meritis gratum me et munem fore. 105
quid uerbis opus est? emi, | atque aduexi heri.
eam me aduexisse nolo resciscat pater.
modo eam reliqui ad portum in naui et seruolum.

sed quid currentem seruom a portu conspicor,
quem naui abire uetui? timeo quid siet. 110

ACANTHIO CHARINVS I.ii

AC. Ex summis opibus uiribusque usque experire, nitere
erus ut minor opera tua seruetur: agedum, Acanthio,
abige aps te lassitudinem, caue pigritiae praeuorteris.
simul enicat suspiritus (uix suffero hercle anhelitum),
simul autem plenis semitis qui aduorsum eunt: aspellito, 115
detrude, deturba in uiam. | haec disciplina hic pessumast:
currenti properanti hau quisquam dignum habet decedere.
ita tres simitu res agendae sunt, quando unam occeperis:
et currendum et pugnandum et autem iurigandum est in uia.
CH. quid illuc est quod ille tam expedite exquirit cursuram sibi? 120
curaest, negoti quid sit aut quid nuntiet. AC. nugas ago.
quam restito, tam maxime res in periclo uortitur.
CH. mali nescioquid nuntiat. AC. genua hunc cursorem deserunt;
perii, seditionem facit lien, occupat praecordia,
perii, animam nequeo uertere, nimi' nihili tibicen siem. 125
numquam edepol omnes balineae mihi hanc lassitudinem eximent. 127
CH. at tu edepol sume laciniam atque apsterge sudorem tibi. 126
AC. domin an foris dicam esse erum Charinum? CHAR. ego animi
                                                              pendeo.
quid illuc sit negoti lubet scire me, †ex hoc metu ut sim certus.†
AC. at etiam asto? at etiam cesso foribus facere hisce assulas? 130
aperite aliquis! ubi Charinus est eru'? domin est an foris?
num quisquam adire ad ostium dignum arbitratur? CH. ecce me,
Acanthio, quem quaeris. AC. nusquamst disciplina ignauior.
   CH. quae te malae res agitant? AC. multae, ere, te atque me.
   CH. quid est negoti? AC. periimus. 135
   CH. principium <id> inimicis dato. 135a
   AC. at tibi sortito id optigit. 136
CH. loquere id negoti quidquid est. AC. placide, uolo adquiescere.
tua caussa rupi ramites, iam dudum sputo sanguinem.
CH. resinam ex melle Aegyptiam uorato, saluom feceris.
AC. at edepol tu calidam picem bibito, aegritudo apscesserit. 140
CH. hominem ego iracundiorem quam te noui neminem.
AC. at ego maledicentiorem quam te noui neminem.

Plautus *Mercator*

CH. sin saluti quod tibi esse censeo, id consuadeo?
AC. apage istiusmodi salutem, <cum> cruciatu quae aduenit.
CH. dic mihi, an boni quid usquamst, quod quisquam uti possiet   145
sine malo omni, aut ne laborem capias quom illo uti uoles?
AC. nescio ego istaec: philosophari numquam didici neque scio.
ego bonum, malum quo accedit, mihi dari hau desidero.
CH. cedo tuam mihi dexteram, agedum, Acanthio. AC. em dabitur,
                                                                                     tene.
CH. uin tu te mihi opsequentem esse an neuis? AC. opera licet   150
experiri, qui me rupi caussa currendo tua,
ut quae scirem scire actutum tibi liceret. CH. liberum
caput tibi faciam <cis> paucos mensis. AC. palpo percutis.
CH egon ausun tibi usquam quicquam facinus falsum proloqui?   154-5
quin iam prius quam sum elocutus, scis sei mentiri uolo. AC. ah!
lassitudinem hercle uerba tua mihi addunt, enicas.
CH. sicine mi opsequens es? AC. quid uis faciam? CH. tun? id quod
                                                                                      uolo.
AC. quid <id> est igitur quod uis? CH. dicam. AC. dice. CH. at enim
                                                                             placide uolo.
AC. dormientis spectatores metuis ne ex somno excites?   160
CH. uae tibi! AC. tibi equidem a portu adporto hoc— CH. quid fers?
                                                                                      dic mihi.
AC. uim metum, cruciatum, curam, iurgiumque atque inopiam.
CH. perii! tu quidem thensaurum huc mi adportauisti mali.
nullus sum. AC. immo es— CH. scio iam, miserum dices tu. AC. dixi
                                                                                     ego tacens.
CH. quid istuc est mali? AC. ne rogites, maxumum infortunium est.
CH. opsecro, dissolue iam me; nimi' diu animi pendeo.   166
AC. placide, multa exquirere etiam priu' uolo quam uapulem.
CH. hercle uero uapulabis, nisi iam loquere aut hinc abis.
AC. hoc sis uide, ut palpatur. nullust, quando occepit, blandior.
CH. opsecro hercle oroque ut istuc quid sit actutum indices,   170
quandoquidem mihi supplicandum seruolo uideo meo.
AC. tandem indignus uideor? CH. immo dignus. AC. Equidem
                                                                                      credidi.
CH. opsecro, num nauis periit? AC. saluast nauis, ne time.
CH. quid alia armamenta? AC. salua et sana sunt. CH. quin tu expedis
quid siet quod me per urbem currens quaerebas modo?   175
AC. tu quidem ex ore orationem mi eripis. CH. taceo. AC. tace.

Plautus *Mercator*

credo, si boni quid ad te nuntiem, instes acriter,
qui nunc, quom malum audiendumst, flagitas me ut eloquar.
CH. opsecro hercle te istuc uti tu mihi malum facias palam.
AC. eloquar, quandoquidem me oras. tuo' pater— CH. quid meu'
　　　　　　　　　　　　　　　　　　　　　　　　　　pater? 180
AC. tuam amicam— CH. quid eam? AC. uidit. CH. uidit? uae
　　　　　　　　　　　　　　　　　　　　　　　　　misero mihi!
hoc quod te rogo responde. AC. quin tu, si quid uis, roga.
CH. qui potuit uidere? | AC. oculis. CH. quo pacto? | AC. hiantibus.
CH. in' hinc dierectus? nugare in re capitali mea.
AC. qui, malum, ego nugor, si tibi quod me rogas respondeo?　　185
CH. certen uidit? AC. tam hercle certe quam ego te aut tu me uides.
CH. ubi eam uidit? AC. intus intra nauim, | ut prope astitit;
et cum ea confabulatust. CH. perdidisti me, pater.
eho tu, eho tu, quin cauisti ne eam uideret, uerbero?
quin, sceleste, | apstrudebas, ne eam conspiceret pater?　　190
AC. quia negotiosi eramus nos nostris negotiis:
armamentis complicandis, componendis studuimus.
dum haec aguntur, lembo aduehitur tuo' pater pauxillulo,
neque quisquam hominem conspicatust, donec in nauim subit.
CH. nequiquam, mare, supterfugi | a tuis tempestatibus:　　195
equidem me iam censebam esse in terra atque in tuto loco,
uerum uideo med ad saxa ferri saeuis fluctibus.
loquere porro, quid sit actum. AC. postquam aspexit mulierem,
rogitare occepit quoia esset. CH. quid respondit? AC. ilico　　199-200
occucurri atque interpello, matri te ancillam tuae
emisse illam. CH. uisun est tibi credere id? AC. etiam rogas?
sed scelestus subigitare occepit. CH. illamne, opsecro?
AC. mirum quin me subigitaret. CH. edepol cor miserum meum,
quod guttatim contabescit, quasi in aquam indideris salem.　　205
perii. AC. em istuc unum uerbum dixisti uerissumum.
stultitia istaec est. CH. quid faciam? credo, non credet pater,
si illam matri meae <me> emisse dicam; post autem mihi
scelu' uidetur, me parenti proloqui mendacium.
neque ille credet, neque credibile est forma eximia mulierem,　　210
eam me emisse ancillam matri. AC. non taces, stultissume?
credet hercle, nam credebat iam mihi. CH. metuo miser,
ne patrem prehendat ut sit gesta res suspicio.
hoc quod te rogo responde, <quaeso>. AC. quaeso, quid rogas?

CH. num esse amicam suspicari uisus est? AC. non uisus est.   215
quin quidque ut dicebam mihi credebat. CH. uerum, ut tibi quidem
uisus est. AC. non, sed credebat. CH. uae mihi misero, nullu' sum!
sed quid ego hic in lamentando pereo, ad nauim non eo?
sequere. AC. si istac ibis, commodum obuiam uenies patri;
postea aspiciet te timidum esse atque exanimatum: ilico   220
retinebit, rogitabit unde illam emeris, quanti emeris:
timidum temptabit te. CH. hac ibo potius. iam censes patrem
abiisse a portu? AC. quin ea ego huc praecucurri gratia,
ne te opprimeret inprudentem atque electaret. CH. optume. —

ACTVS II

DEMIPHO   II.i

Miris modis di ludos faciunt hominibus   225
mirisque exemplis somnia in somnis danunt.
uelut ego nocte hac quae praeteriit proxuma
in somnis egi satis et fui homo exercitus.
mercari uisus mihi sum formosam capram;
ei ne noceret quam domi ante habui capram   230
neu discordarent si ambae in uno essent loco,
posterius quam mercatus fueram uisu' sum
in custodelam simiae concredere.
ea simia adeo post hau multo ad me uenit,
male mihi precatur et facit conuicium: 235
ait sese illius opera atque aduentu caprae
flagitium et damnum fecisse hau mediocriter;
dicit capram, quam dederam seruandam sibi,
suai uxoris dotem ambedisse oppido.
mi illud uideri mirum, ut una illaec capra   240
uxoris simiai dotem ambederit.
instare factum simia atque hoc denique
respondet, ni properem illam ab sese abducere,
ad me domum intro ad uxorem ducturum meam.
atque oppido hercle bene uelle illi uisu' sum,   245
ast non habere quoi commendarem capram;
quo magi' quid facerem cura cruciabar miser.
interea ad me haedus uisust adgredirier,

infit mihi praedicare sese ab simia
capram abduxisse et coepit inridere me; 250
ego enim lugere atque abductam illam aegre pati.
hoc quam ad rem credam pertinere somnium,
nequeo inuenire; nisi capram illam suspicor
iam me inuenisse quae sit aut quid uoluerit.
ad portum hinc abii mane cum luci semul; 255
postquam id quod uolui transegi, atque ego conspicor
nauim ex Rhodo quast heri aduectus filius;
conlibitumst illuc mihi nescioqui uisere:
inscendo in lembum; | atque ad nauim deuehor.
atque ego illi aspicio forma eximia mulierem, 260
filiu' quam aduexit meu' matri ancillam suae.
quam ego postquam aspexi, non ita amo ut sanei solent
homines, sed eodem pacto ut insanei solent.
amaui hercle equidem ego olim in adulescentia,
uerum ad hoc exemplum numquam ut nunc insanio. 265
unum quidem hercle iam scio, periisse me;
uosmet uidete ceterum quanti siem.
nunc hoc profecto sic est: haec illast capra;
uerum hercle simia illa atque haedus mihi malum
adportant, atque eos esse quos dicam hau scio. 270
sed conticiscam, nam eccum it uicinus foras.

LYSIMACHVS DEMIPHO SERVVS   II.ii

LY. Profecto ego illunc hircum castrari uolo,
ruri qui uobeis exhibet negotium.
DE. nec omen illuc mihi nec auspicium placet.
quasi hircum metuo ne uxor me castret mea. 275
atque illius hic nunc simiae partis ferat.
LY. i tu hinc ad uillam atque istos rastros uilico
Pisto ipsi facito coram ut tradas in manum.
uxori facito ut nunties, negotium
mihi esse in urbe, ne me exspectet; nam mihi 280
tris hodie litis iudicandas dicito.
ei, et hoc memento adicere. SE. numquid amplius?
LY. tantumst. DE. Lysimache, salue. | LY. eugae, Demipho,
salueto. quid agis? quid fit? DE. quod miserrumus.

LY. di melius faxint! DE. di hoc quidem faciunt. LY. quid
　　　　　　　　　　　　　　　　　　　　　　　　est? 285
DE. dicam, si uideam tibi | esse operam aut otium.
LY. quamquam negotiumst, si quid ueis, Demipho,
non sum occupatus umquam amico operam dare.
DE. benignitatem tuam mi experto praedicas.
quid tibi ego aetatis uideor? LY. Accherunticus,　　290
senex uetus, decrepitus. DE. peruorse uides.
puer sum, Lysimache, septuennis. LY. sanun es,
qui puerum te esse dicas? DE. uera praedico.
LY. modo hercle in mentem uenit, quid tu diceres:
senex quom extemplo est, iam nec sentit nec sapit,　　295
aiunt solere eum rusum repuerascere.
DE. immo bis tanto ualeo quam ualui prius.
LY. bene hercle factum, et gaudeo. DE. immo si scias,
oculeis quoque etiam plus iam uideo quam prius.
LY. benest. DE. malae rei deico. LY. iam istuc non benest.
DE. sed ausimne ego tibi eloqui fideliter?　　301
LY. audacter. DE. animum aduorte. LY. fiet sedulo.
DE. hodie ire in ludum occepi litterarium,
Lysimache. ternas scio iam. LY. quid ternas? DE. amo.
LY. tun capite cano amas, senex nequissume?　　305
DE. si canum seu istuc rutilumst siue atrumst, amo.
LY. ludificas nunc tu me heic, opinor, Demipho.
DE. decide collum stanti, si falsum loquor;
uel, ut scias me amare, cape cultrum, ac seca
digitum uel aurem uel tu nassum uel labrum:　　310
sei mouero me seu secari sensero,
Lysimache, auctor sum ut tu me amando— | enices.
LY. si umquam uidistis pictum amatorem, em illic est.
nam meo quidem animo uetulus, decrepitus senex
tantidemst quasi sit signum pictum in pariete.　　315
DE. nunc tu me, credo, castigare cogitas.
LY. egon te? DE. nihil est iam quod tu mihi suscenseas:
fecere tale ante aliei spectatei uirei.
peccare humanumst, humanum autem ignoscere est:
humanum amarest atque id ui optingit deum.　　320
ne sis me obiurga, hoc non uoluntas me impulit.
LY. quin non obiurgo. DE. at ne deteriorem tamen

hoc facto ducas. LY. egon te? ah, ne di siuerint!
DE. uide sis modo etiam. LY. uisumst. DE. certen?
                                            LY. perdi' me.
hic homo ex amore insanit. numquid uis? DE. uale.   325
LY. ad portum propero, nam ibi mihi negotium est.
DE. bene ambulato. LY. bene uale.— DE. bene sit tibi.
quin mihi quoque etiamst ad portum negotium.
nunc adeo ibo illuc. sed optume gnatum meum
uideo eccum. opperiar hominem. hoc nunc mihi uiso opust,
huic persuadere quo modo potis siem,   331
ut illam uendat neue det matri suae;
nam ei dono aduexe audiui. sed praecauto opust,
ne hic illam me animum adiecisse aliqua sentiat.

CHARINVS DEMIPHO   II.iii

CH. Homo me miserior nullust aeque, opinor,   335
neque aduorsa quoi plura sint sempiterna;
satin quidquid est, quam rem agere occepi,
proprium nequit mi euenire quod cupio?
ita mihi mala res aliqua obicitur,
bonum quae meum comprimit consilium.   340
miser amicam mihi paraui, | animi caussa, pretio eripui,
ratus clam patrem <me> meum posse habere:
is resciuit et uidit et perdidit me;
neque is quom roget quid loquar cogitatumst,
ita animi decem in pectore incerti certant.   345
nec quid corde nunc consili capere possim
scio, tantus cum cura meost error animo,
dum serui mei perplacet mi consilium,
dum rursum hau placet nec pater poti' uidetur
induci ut putet matri ancillam emptam esse illam.   350
nunc si dico ut res est atque illam mihi me
emisse indico, quem ad modum existumet me?
atque illam apstrahat, trans mare hinc uenum asportet;
scio saeuo' quam sit, domo doctus. igitur   354-355
hoccine est amare? arare mauelim quam sic amare.
iam hinc olim inuitum domo extrusit ab se,
mercatum ire iussit: ibi hoc malum ego inueni.
ubi uoluptatem aegritudo uincat, quid ibi inest amoeni?

Plautus *Mercator*

nequiquam abdidi, apscondidi, apstrusam habebam: 360
muscast meu' pater, nil potest clam illum haberi,
nec sacrum nec tam profanum quicquamst quin ibi ilico adsit.
nec, qui rebus meis confidam mi ulla spes in corde certast.
DE. quid illuc est quod solus secum fabulatur filius?
sollicitus mihi nescioqua re uidetur. CH. attatae! 365
meu' pater hicquidem est quem uideo. ibo, adloquar. quid fit,
pater?
DE. unde incedis, quid festinas, gnate mi? CH. recte, pater.
DE. ita uolo, sed istuc quid est tibi quod commutatust color?
numquid tibi dolet? CH. nescioquid meo animost aegre, pater.
poste hac nocte non quieui sati' mea ex sententia. 370
DE. ergo edepol palles. si sapias, eas ac decumbas domi. 373
CH. otium non est: mandatis rebus praeuorti uolo.
DE. cras agito, perendie agito. CH. saepe ex te audiui, pater:
rei mandatae omnis sapientis primum praeuorti decet. 376
DE. age igitur; nolo aduorsari tuam aduorsum sententiam.
CH. saluos sum, siquidem isti dicto solida et perpetuast fides.
DE. quid illuc est quod ille a me solus se in consilium
seuocat?
non uereor ne illam me amare hic potuerit rescicere; 380
quippe haud etiam quicquam inepte feci, amantes ut solent.
CH. res adhuc quidem hercle in tutost, nam hunc nescire sat
scio
de illa amica; quod si sciret, esset alia oratio.
DE. quin ego hunc adgredior de illa? CH. quin ego hinc me
amolior?
eo ego, ut quae mandata amicus amicis tradam. DE. immo
mane; 385
paucula etiam sciscitare priu' uolo. CH. dic quid uelis.
DE. usquine ualuisti? CH. perpetuo recte, dum quidem illic
fui;
uerum in portum huc ut sum aduectus, nescioqui animus mihi
dolet.
DE. nausea edepol factum credo; uerum actutum apscesserit.
sed quid ais? ecquam tu aduexti tuae matri ancillam e Rhodo?
CH. aduexi. DE. quid? ea ut uidetur mulier? CH. non edepol
mala. 391

DE. ut moratast? CH. nullam uidi melius mea sententia.
DE. mihi quidem edepol uisast quom illam uidi— CH. eho an
              uidisti, pater?
DE. uidi. uerum non ex usu nostrost, neque adeo placet.
CH. qui uero? DE. quia—<quia> non nostra formam habet
             dignam domo. 395
nihil opust nobis ancilla nisi quae texat, quae molat,
lignum caedat, pensum faciat, aedis uorrat, uapulet,
quae habeat cottidianum familiae coctum cibum:
horunc illa nihilum quicquam facere poterit. CH. admodum.
ea caussa equidem illam emi, dono quam darem matri meae.
DE. ne duas neue te aduexisse dixeris. CH. di me
           adiuuant. 401-402
DE. labefacto paulatim. uerum quod praeterii dicere,
neque illa matrem satis honeste tuam sequi poterit comes
neque sinam. CH. qui uero? DE. quia illa forma matrem
             familias 405
flagitium sit sei sequatur; quando incedat per uias,
contemplent, conspiciant omnes, nutent, nictent, sibilent,
uellicent, uocent, molesti sint; occentent ostium:
impleantur elegeorum meae fores carbonibus. 409
atque, ut nunc sunt maledicentes homines, uxori meae
mihique obiectent lenocinium facere. Nam| quid eost opus?
CH. hercle qui tu recte dicis et tibi | adsentior.
sed quid illa nunc fiet? DE. recte. ego emero matri tuae
ancillam uiraginem aliquam non malam, forma mala,
ut matrem addecet familias, aut Syram aut Aegyptiam: 415
ea molet, coquet, conficiet pensum, pinsetur flagro,
neque propter eam quicquam eueniet nostris foribus flagiti.
CH. quid si igitur reddatur illi unde empta est? DE. Minime
             gentium.
CH. dixit se redhibere si non placeat. DE. nihil istoc opust:
litigari nolo ego usquam, tuam autem accusari fidem; 420
multo edepol, si quid faciendumst, facere damni mauolo
quam opprobramentum aut flagitium muliebre ecferri domo.
me tibi illam posse opinor luculente uendere.
CH. dum quidem hercle ne minoris uendas quam ego emi,
             pater. 424-425

DE. tace modo: senex est quidam, qui illam mandauit mihi
ut emerem— | ad istanc faciem. | CH. at mihi quidam
                                             adulescens, pater,
mandauit ad illam faciem, | ita ut illa est, emerem sibi.
DE. uiginti minis opinor posse me illam uendere.
CH. at ego si uelim, iam dantur septem et uiginti minae. 430
DE. at ego— CH. quin ego, inquam— DE. ah, nescis quid
                                             dicturus sum, tace.
tris minas accudere etiam possum, ut triginta sient.
CH. quo uortisti? DE. ad illum qui emit. CH. ubinamst is
                                                homo gentium?
DE. eccillum uideo. iubet quinque me addere etiam nunc
                                                minas. 434-435
CH. hercle illunc di | infelicent, quisquis est. DE. ibidem
                                                          mihi
etiam nunc adnutat addam sex minas. CH. septem mihi.
DE. numquam edepol me uincet hodie. CH. commodis poscit,
                                                        pater.
DE. nequiquam poscit: ego habebo. CH. at illic pollicitust
                                                        prior.
DE. nihili facio. CH. quinquaginta poscit. DE. non centum
                                                   datur. 440
potine ut ne licitere aduorsum <mei> animi sententiam?
maxumam hercle habebis praedam: ita ille est, quoi emitur,
                                                        senex;
sanus non est ex amore | illius. quod posces feres.
CH. certe edepol adulescens ille, quoi ego emo, ecflictim
                                                        perit
eius amore. DE. multo hercle ille magi' senex, si tu scias. 445
CH. numquam edepol fuit neque fiet ille senex insanior
ex amore quam ille adulescens quoi ego do hanc operam,
                                                        pater.
DE. quiesce, inquam. istanc rem ego recte uidero. CH. Quid
                                                ais? DE. quid est?
CH. non ego illam mancupio accepi. DE. sed ille illam
                                                accipiet. sine.
CH. non potes tu lege uendere illam. DE. ego aliquid
                                                uidero. 450
CH. post autem communest illa mihi cum alio. qui scio

quid sit ei animi, uenirene eam uelit an non uelit?
DE. ego scio uelle. CH. at pol ego esse credo aliquem qui non
uelit.
DE. quid id mea refert? CH. quia illi suam rem esse aequomst
in manu.
DE. quid ais? CH. communis mihi illa est cum illo: is hic
nunc non adest. 455
DE. priu' respondes quam rogo. CH. priu' tu emis quam
uendo, pater.
nescio, inquam, uelit ille illam necne abalienarier.
DE. quid? illi quoidam qui mandauit tibi si emetur, tum uolet,
si ego emo illi qui mandauit, tum ille nolet? nihil agis.
numquam edepol quisquam illam habebit potius quam ille
quem ego uolo. 460
CH. certumnest? DE. censen certum esse? quin ad nauim iam
hinc eo,
ibi uenibit. CH. uin me tecum illo ire? DE. nolo. CH. non
places.
DE. meliust te, quae sunt mandatae res tibi, praeuortier.
CH. tu prohibes. DE. at me incusato: te fecisse sedulo.
ad portum ne bitas, dico iam tibi. CH. auscultabitur.   465
DE. ibo ad portum. ne hic resciscat cauto opust: non ipse
emam,
sed Lysimacho amico mandabo. is se ad portum dixerat
ire dudum. me moror quom heic asto.— CH. nullus sum,
occidi.

CHARINVS EVTYCHVS   II.iv

CH. Pentheum diripuisse aiunt Bacchas: nugas maxumas
fuisse credo, praeut quo pacto | ego diuorsus distrahor.   470
qur ego ueiuo? qur non morior? quid mihist in uita boni?
certumst, ibo ad medicum atque ibi me toxico morti dabo,
quando id mi adimitur qua caussa uitam cupio uiuere.
EV. mane, mane opsecro, Charine. CH. quis me reuocat?
EV. Eutychus,
tuos amicus et sodalis, simul uicinus proxumus.   475
CH. non tu scis quantum malarum rerum sustineam. EV. scio;
omnia ego istaec auscultaui ab ostio, omnem rem scio.
CH. quid id est quod scis? EV. tuo' pater uolt uendere—

CH. omnem rem tenes.
EV. tuam amicam. CH. nimium multum scis.
EV. tui ingratieis. 479
CH. plurumum tu scis. sed qui scis esse amicam illam meam?
EV. tute heri ipsus mihi narrasti. CH. satine ut oblitus fui
tibi me narrauisse? EV. hau mirumst factum. CH. te nunc
consulo.
responde: quo leto censes me ut peream potissumum?
EV. non taces? caue tu istuc deixis. CH. quid ueis me igitur
deicere?
EV uin patri sublinere pulchre me os tuo? CH. sane uolo. 485
EV. uisne eam ad portum— CH. qui potius quam uoles?
EV. atque eximam
mulierem pretio? CH. qui potius quam auro expendas?
EV. unde erit?
CH. Achillem orabo, aurum mihi det Hector qui expensus
fuit.
EV. sanun es? CH. pol sanus sei sim, non te medicum mi
expetam. 489
EV. tanti quanti poscit, uin tanti illam emi? | CH. auctarium
adicito uel mille nummum plus quam poscet. EV. iam tace.
sed quid ais? unde erit argentum quod des, quom poscet
pater?
CH. inuenietur, exquiretur, aliquid fiet; enicas.
EV. iam istuc "aliquid fiet" metuo. CH. quin taces?
EV. Muto imperas.
CH. satin istuc mandatumst? EV. potin ut aliud cures?
CH. non potest. 495
EV. bene uale. CH. non edepol possum priu' quam tu ad me
redieris.
EV. melius sanus sis. CH. uale, uince et me serua. EV. ego
fecero.
domi maneto me. CH. ergo actutum face cum praeda
recipias.

ACTVS III

LYSIMACHVS PASICOMPSA III.i

LY. Amice amico operam dedi: uicinus quod rogauit,
hoc emi mercimonium. mea es tu, sequere sane.   500
ne plora: nimis stulte facis, oculos corrumpis talis.
quin tibi quidem quod rideas magis est, quam ut lamentere.
PA. amabo ecastor, mi senex, eloquere-- LY. exquire quiduis.
PA. qur emeris me. LY. tene ego? ut quod imperetur facias,
item quod tu mihi si imperes, ego faciam. PA. facere certumst.
pro copia et sapientia quae te uelle arbitrabor.   506
LY. laboriossi nil tibi quicquam operis imperabo.
PA. namque edepol equidem, mi senex, non didici baiiolare
nec pecua ruri pascere nec pueros nutricare.
LY. bona si esse uis, bene erit tibi. PA. tum pol ego perii
             misera. 510
LY. qui? PA. quia illim unde huc aduecta sum, malis bene
            esse solitumst.
<LY. sed hic bonis. PA. tum mulieri bene esse poterit
             nulli.> 511a
LY. quasi deicas nullam mulierem bonam esse. PA. haud
            equidem deico
nec mos meust ut praedicem quod ego omnis scire credam.
LY. oratio edepol pluris est huius quam quanti haec emptast.
rogare hoc unum te uolo. PA. roganti respondebo.   515
LY. quid ais tu? quid nomen tibi deicam esse?
PA. Pasicompsae.
LY. ex forma nomen inditumst. sed quid ais, Pasicompsa?
possin tu, sei ussus uenerit, subtemen tenue nere?
PA. possum. LY. sei tenue scis, scio te uberius posse nere.
PA. de lanificio neminem metuo, una aetate quae sit.   520
LY. bonae hercle te frugi arbitror, matura iam inde aetate
quom scis facere officium tuom, mulier. PA. pol docta didici.
operam accusari non sinam meam. LY. em istaec hercle res
             est.
ouem tibi eccillam dabo, natam annos sexaginta,   524
peculiarem. PA. mi senex, tam uetulam? LY. generis graecist;
eam sei curabis, perbonast, tondetur nimium scite.

Plautus *Mercator*

PA. honoris caussa quidquid est quod dabitur gratum habebo.
LY. nunc, mulier, ne tu frustra sis, mea non es, ne arbitrere.
PA. dic igitur quaeso, quoia sum? LY. tuo ero redempta's
    rursum;
ego te redemi, | ille mecum orauit. PA. animus rediit,   530
sei mecum seruatur fides. LY. bono animo es, liberabit
ille te homo: ita edepol deperit, atque hodie primum uidit.
PA. ecastor iam bienniumst quom mecum rem coëpit.
nunc, quando amicum te scio | esse illius, indicabo.
LY. quid ais tu? iam bienniumst quom tecum rem habet?
    PA. certo; 535
et inter nos coniurauimus, ego cum illo et ille mecum:
ego cum uiro et ill' cum muliere, nisi cum illo aut ille
    mecum, 536a
neuter stupri caussa caput limaret. LY. di immortales!
etiam cum uxore non cubet? PA. amabo, | an maritust?
neque est neque erit. LY. nolim quidem. | homo hercle
    peiierauit.
PA. nullum adulescentem plus amo. LY. puer est ille quidem,
    stulta. 540
nam illi quidem hau sane diust quom dentes exciderunt.
PA. quid, dentes? LY. nihil est. sequere sis. hunc me diem
    unum orauit
ut apud me praehiberem locum, | ideo quia uxor rurist.—

DEMIPHO   III.ii

DE. Tandem impetraui ut egomet me corrumperem:
emptast amica clam uxorem et clam filium.   545
certumst, antiqua recolam et seruibo mihi.
breue iam relicuom uitae spatiumst: quin ego
uoluptate, uino et amore delectauero.
nam hanc se bene habere aetatem nimiost aequius.
adulescens quom sis, tum quom est sanguis integer,   550
rei tuae quaerundae conuenit operam dare;
demum igitur quom sis iam senex, tum in otium
te conloces, dum potest ames: id iam lucrumst
quod uiuis. hoc ut deico, facteis persequar.
nunc tamen interea ad med huc inuisam domum: 555

uxor me exspectat iam dudum essuriens domi;
iam iurgio enicabit, si intro rediero.
uerum hercle postremo, utut est, non ibo tamen,
sed hunc uicinum priu' conueniam quam domum
redeam; ut mihi aedis aliquas conducat uolo, 560
ubi habitet istaec mulier. atque eccum it foras.

LYSIMACHVS DEMIPHO III.iii

LY. Adducam ego illum iam ad te, si conuenero.
DE. me dicit. LY. quid ais, Demipho? DE. est mulier domi?
LY. quid censes? DE. quid si uisam? LY. quid properas?
<mane.>
DE. quid faciam? LY. quod opust facto facito ut cogites. 565
DE. quid cogitem? equidem hercle opus hoc facto existumo,
ut illo intro eam. LY. itane uero, ueruex? intro eas?
DE. quid aliud faciam? LY. prius hoc ausculta, atque ades:
prius etiamst quod te facere ego aequom censeo.
nam nunc si illo intro ieris, amplecti uoles, 570
confabulari atque ausculari. DE. tu quidem
meum animum gestas: scis quid acturus siem.
LY. peruorse facies. DE. quodne amem? LY. tanto minus.
iaiunitatis plenus, anima foetida,
senex hircosus tu osculere mulierem? 575
utine adueniens uomitum excutias mulieri?
scio pol te amare, quom istaec praemostras mihi.
DE. quid si igitur unum faciam hoc? si censes, coquom
aliquem arripiamus, prandium qui percoquat
apud te hic usque ad uesperum. LY. em istuc censeo. 580
nunc tu sapienter loquere neque amatorie.
DE. quid stamus? quin ergo imus atque opsonium
curamus, pulchre ut simus? LY. equidem te sequor.
atque hercle inuenies tu locum illi, si sapis:
nullum hercle praeter hunc diem illa apud med erit. 585
metuo ego uxorem, cras si rure redierit
ne illam hic offendat. DE. res parata est, sequere me.—

CHARINVS EVTYCHVS III.iv

CH. Sumne ego homo miser, qui nusquam bene queo
                                       quiescere?
si domi sum, foris est animus, sin foris sum, animus domist.
ita mi in pectore atque in corde facit amor incendium: 590
ni ex oculis lacrumae defendant, iam ardeat credo caput.
spem teneo, salutem amisi; redeat an non nescio:
si opprimit pater quod dixit, exsolatum abiit salus;
sein sodalis quod promisit fecit, non abiit salus.
sed tamendem si podagrosis pedibus esset Eutychus,   595
iam a portu rediisse potuit. id illi uitium maxumumst,
quod nimi' tardus est aduorsum mei animi sententiam.
sed isne est, quem currentem uideo? | ipsus est. ibo obuiam.
nunc, quod restat,--ei disperii! uoltus ne utiquam huius placet;
tristis incedit (pectus ardet, haereo), quassat caput.   600
Eutyche! EV eu, Charine! CH. priu' quam recipias anhelitum,
uno uerbo eloquere: ubi ego sum? | hicine an apud mortuos?
EV. neque apud mortuos neque hic es. CH. saluos sum,
                                       inmortalitas
mihi data est: hic emit illam, pulchre os subleuit patri.
impetrabilior qui uiuat nullus est. dice, opsecro: 605
sei neque hic neque Accherunti sum, ubi sum? EV. nusquam
                                       gentium.
CH. disperii, illaec interemit me modo | oratio.
EV. odiosast oratio, quom rem agas longinquom loqui.
CH. quidquid est, ad capita rerum perueni. EV. primum
omnium: periimus. CH. quin tu illud potius nuntias quod
                                       nescio? 610
EV. mulier alienata est aps te. | CH. Eutyche, capital facis.
EV. qui? CH. quia aequalem et sodalem, liberum ciuem,
enicas.
EV. ne di sierint. CH. demisisti gladium in iugulum: iam
                                       cadam.
EV. quaeso hercle, animum ne desponde. CH. nullust quem
                                     despondeam. 614
loquere porro aliam malam rem. quoii est empta? EV. nescio.
iam addicta atque abducta erat, quom ad portum uenio.

Plautus *Mercator*

CH. uae mihi!
montis tu quidem mali in me ardentis iam dudum iacis.   617
perge, excrucia, carnufex, quandoquidem occepisti semel.618
EV. quid ego feci? CH. perdidisti me et fidem mecum
tuam.   625
EV. di sciunt culpam meam istanc non esse ullam. |
CH. eugepae!   626
deos absentis testis memoras: qui ego istuc credam tibi?   627
EV. quia tibi in manu est quod credas, ego quod dicam, id
mihi in manust.   628
CH. de istac re | argutus es, ut par pari respondeas,
ad mandata claudus, caecus, mutus, mancus, debilis.
promittebas te os sublinere meo patri: egomet credidi
homini docto rem mandare, is lapidi mando maxumo.
EV. quid ego facerem? CH. quid tu faceres? men rogas?
requireres,
rogitares quis esset aut unde esset, qua prosapia,   634
ciuisne esset an peregrinus. EV. ciuem esse aibant Atticum.
CH. ubi habitaret inuenires saltem, si nomen nequis.
EV. nemo aiebat scire. CH. at saltem | hominis faciem
exquireres.
EV. feci. CH. qua forma esse aiebant, <Eutyche>?
EV. ego dicam tibi:
canum, uarum, uentriosum, bucculentum, breuiculum,
subnigris oculis, oblongis malis, pansam aliquantulum.   640
CH. non hominem mihi, sed thensaurum nescioquem
memoras mali.
numquid est quod dicas aliud de illo? EV. tantum, quod
sciam.
CH. edepol ne ille oblongis malis mihi dedit magnum malum.
non possum durare, certumst exsulatum hinc ire me.
sed quam capiam ciuitatem, cogito, potissumum: 645
Megares, Eretriam, Corinthum, Chalcidem, Cretam, Cyprum,
Sicyonem, Cnidum, Zacynthum, Lesbiam, Boeotiam.
EV. qur istuc coeptas consilium? CH. quia enim me adflictat
amor.
EV. quid tu ais? quid quom illuc quo nunc ire paritas ueneris,
si ibi amare forte occipias atque item eius sit inopia,   650
iam inde porro aufugies, deinde item illinc, si item euenerit?

quis modus tibi exsilio tandem eueniet, qui finis fugae?
quae patria aut domus tibi stabilis esse poterit? dic mihi.
cedo, si hac urbe abis, amorem te hic relicturum putas?
si id fore ita sat animo acceptum est, certum id, pro certo si
                                        habes, 655
quanto te satiust rus aliquo abire, ibi esse, ibi uiuere
adeo dum illius te cupiditas atque amor missum facit?
CH. iam dixisti? EV. dixi. CH. frustra dixti. hoc mihi
                                    certissumumst.
eo domum, patrem atque matrem ut meos salutem, postea
clam patrem patria hac ecfugiam, aut aliquid capiam
                                    consili.— 660
EV. ut corripuit se repente atque abiit! heu misero mihi!
si ille abierit, mea factum omnes dicent esse ignauia.
certumst praeconum iubere iam quantum est conducier,
qui illam inuestigent, qui inueniant. post ad praetorem ilico
ibo, orabo ut conquaestores det mi in uicis omnibus;   665
nam mihi nil relicti quicquam | aliud iam esse intellego.—

ACTVS IV

DORIPPA SYRA   IV.i

DO. Quoniam a uiro ad me rus aduenit nuntius
rus non iturum, feci ego ingenium meum,
reueni, ut illum persequar qui me fugit.
sed anum non uideo consequi nostram Syram.   670
atque eccam incedit tandem. quin is ocius?
SY. nequeo mecastor, tantum hoc onerist quod fero.
DO. quid oneris? SY. annos octoginta et quattuor;
et eodem accedit seruitus, sudor, sitis:
simul haec quae porto deprimunt. DO. aliquid cedo   675
†qui hanc uicini nostri aram augeam.†
da sane hanc uirgam lauri. abi tu intro. SY. eo.—
DO. Apollo, quaeso te ut des pacem propitius,
salutem et sanitatem nostrae familiae,
meoque ut parcas gnato pace propitius.   680
SY. disperii, perii misera, uae miserae mihi!
DO. satin tu sana's, opsecro? quid eiulas?

SY. Dorippa, mea Dorippa. DO. quid clamas, opsecro?
SY. nescioquaest mulier intus hic in aedibus.
DO. quid, mulier? SY. mulier meretrix. DO. ueron serio? 685
SY. nimium scis sapere ruri quae non manseris.
quamuis insipiens poterat persentiscere
<illum non temere hic mansisse. ecastor palamst> 687a
illam esse amicam tui uiri bellissumi.
DO. credo mecastor. SY. ei hac mecum, ut uideas semul
tuam Alcumenam paelicem, Iuno mea.— 690
DO. ecastor uero istuc eo quantum potest.—

LYSIMACHVS IV.ii

LY. Parumne est malai rei, quod amat Demipho,
ni sumptuosus insuper etiam siet?
decem si uocasset summos ad cenam uiros,
nimium opsonauit. sed coquos, quasi in mari 695
solet hortator remiges hortarier,
ita hortabatur. egomet conduxi coquom.
sed eum demiror non uenire ut iusseram.
sed quinam hinc a nobis exit? aperitur foris.

DORIPPA LYSIMACHVS IV.iii

DO. Miserior mulier me nec fiet nec fuit, 700
tali uiro quae nupserim. heu miserae mihi!
em quoi te et tua, quae tu habeas, commendes uiro,
em quoi decem talenta dotis detuli,
haec ut uiderem, ut ferrem has contumelias!
LY. perii hercle! rure iam rediit uxor mea: 705
uidisse credo mulierem <illam> in aedibus.
sed quae loquatur exaudire hinc non queo.
accedam propius. DO. uae miserae mi! LY. immo mihi.
DO. disperii! | LY. equidem hercle oppido perii miser!
uidit. ut te omnes, Demipho, di perduint! 710
DO. pol hoc est, ire quod rus meu' uir noluit.
LY. quid nunc ego faciam nisi uti adeam atque adloquar?
iubet saluere suo' uir uxorem suam.
urbani fiunt rustici? DO. pudicius

faciunt, quam | illi qui non fiunt rustici. 715
LY. num quid delinquont rustici? DO. ecastor minus
quam urbani, et multo minu' mali quaerunt sibi.
LY. quid autem urbani deliquerunt? dic mihi,
cupio hercle scire. DO. sed tu me temptas sciens. 721
quoia illa mulier intust? LY. uidistine eam? 719
DO. uidi. LY. quoia ea sit rogitas? DO. resciscam tamen. 720
LY. uin dicam quoiast? illa—illa edepol—uae mihi! 722
nescio quid dicam. DO. haeres. | LY. hau uidi magis.
DO. quin dicis? LY. quin si liceat— DO. dictum oportuit.
LY. non possum, ita instas; urges quasi pro noxio. 725
DO. scio, innoxiu's. LY. audacter quam uis dicito.
DO. dice igitur. LY. dicam. | DO. atqui dicundum est tamen.
LY. illast— etiam uis nomen dicam? DO. nihil agis,
manufesto teneo in noxia. LY. qua noxia?
istaquidem illa est. DO. quae illa est? LY. illa— DO. †iohia†
LY. iam— si nihil usus esset, iam non dicerem. 731
DO. non tu scis quae sit illa? | LY. immo iam scio: 732-735
de istac sum iudex captus. DO. iudex? iam scio:
nunc tu in consilium istam aduocauisti tibi.
LY. immo sic: sequestro mihi datast. DO. intellego.
LY. nihil hercle istius quicquam est. DO. numero purigas.
LY. nimium negoti repperi. enim uero haereo. 740

COCVS LYSIMACHVS DORIPPA SYRA   IV.iv

CO. Agite ite actutum, nam mi amatori seni
coquendast cena. | atque, quom recogito,
nobis coquendast, non <quoi con>ducti sumus.
nam qui amat quod amat si habet, id habet pro cibo:
uidere, amplecti, | osculari, | adloqui; 745
sed nos confido onustos redituros domum.
eite hac. sed eccum qui nos conduxit senex.
LY. ecce autem perii, coquos adest! CO. aduenimus.
LY. abei. CO. quid, abeam? LY. st! abei. | CO. abeam? |
                                                        LY. abei.
CO. non estis cenaturi? LY. iam saturi sumus. 750
CO. sed— LY. interii! DO. quid ais tu? etiamne haec illi tibi
iusserunt ferri, quos inter iudex datu's?

Plautus *Mercator*

CO. haecin tua est amica, quam dudum mihi
te amare dixtei, quom opsonabas? LY. non taces?
CO. sati' scitum filum mulieris. uerum hercle anet. 755
LY. abin dierectus? CO. hau malast. LY. at tu malu's.
CO. scitam hercle opinor concubinam hanc. LY. non abis?
non ego sum qui te dudum conduxi. CO. quid est?
immo hercle tu istic ipsus. LY. uae misero mihi!
CO. nempe uxor rurist tua, quam dudum deixeras 760
te odisse atque anguis. LY. egone istuc dixi tibi?
CO. mihi quidem hercle. | LY. ita me amabit Iuppiter,
uxor, ut ego illud numquam deixi. DO. etiam negas?
palam istaec fiunt te me odisse. LY. quin nego.
CO. non, non ted odisse aibat, sed uxorem suam; 765
et uxorem suam ruri esse aiebat. LY. haec east.
quid mihi molestu's? CO. quia nouisse me negas;
nisi metuis tu istanc. LY. sapio, nam mihi unicast.
CO. uein me experirei? LY. nolo. CO. mercedem cedo.
LY. cras petito; dabitur. nunc abi. DO. heu miserae mihi! 770
LY. nunc ego uerum illud uerbum esse experior uetus:
aliquid mali esse propter uicinum malum.
CO. qur heic astamus? quin abimus? †incommodi†
si quid tibi euenit, id non est culpa mea.
LY. quin me eradicas miserum. CO. scio iam quid uelis: 775
nemp' me hinc abire ueis. LY. uolo inquam. CO. abibitur.
drachmam dato. LY. dabitur. CO. darei ergo sis iube.
darei potest interea dum illei ponunt. LY. quin abis?
potine ut molestus ne sis? CO. agite apponite
opsonium istuc ante pedes illi seni. 780
haec uassa aut mox aut cras iubebo aps te peti.
sequimini.— LY. fortasse te illum mirari coquom
quod uenit atque haec attulit. dicam quid est.
DO. non miror sei quid damni facis aut flagiti.
nec pol ego patiar seic me nuptam tam male 785
measque in aedis sic scorta obductarier.
Syra, i, rogato meum patrem uerbeis meeis,
ut ueniat ad me iam simul tecum. | — SY. eo.—
LY. nescis negoti quid sit, uxor, obsecro.
concepteis uerbeis iam iusiurandum dabo 790
me numquam quicquam cum illa— iamne abiit Syra?

perii hercle! ecce autem haec abiit. uae misero mihi!
at te, uicine, di deaeque perduint,
cum tua | amica cumque amationibus!
suspicione impleuit me indignissume, 795
conciuit hostis domi: uxor acerrumast.
ibo ad forum atque Demiphoni haec eloquar,
me istanc capillo protracturum esse in uiam,
nisi hinc abducit quo uolt ex hisce aedibus.
uxor, heus uxor! quamquam tu irata es mihi, 800
iubeas, si sapias, haec <hinc> intro auferrier:
eadem licebit mox cenare rectius.—

SYRA EVTYCHVS   IV.v

SY. Era quo me misit, ad patrem, non est domi:
rus abiisse aibant. nunc domum renuntio.
EV. defessus sum urbem totam peruenarier: 805
nihil inuestigo quicquam de illa muliere.
sed mater rure rediit, nam uideo Syram
astare ante aedis. Syra! SY. quis est qui me uocat?
EV. erus atque alumnus tuo' sum. SY. salue, alumnule.
EV. iam mater rure rediit? responde mihi. 810
SY. cum quidem salute familiai maxuma.
EV. quid istuc negotist? SY. tuo' pater bellissumus
amicam adduxit intro in aedis. EV. quo modo?
SY. adueniens mater rure eam offendit domi.
EV. pol haud censebam istarum esse operarum patrem. 815
etiam nunc mulier intust? SY. etiam. EV. sequere me.—

SYRA   IV.vi

SY. Ecastor lege dura uiuont mulieres
multoque iniquiore miserae quam uiri.
nam si uir scortum duxit clam uxorem suam,
id si resciuit uxor, inpunest uiro; 820
uxor uirum si clam domo egressa est foras,
uiro fit caussa, exigitur matrumonio.
utinam lex esset eadem quae uxori est uiro;
nam uxor contenta est, quae bona est, uno uiro:

qui minu' uir una uxore contentus siet? 825
ecastor faxim, si itidem plectantur uiri,
si quis clam uxorem duxerit scortum suam,
ut illae exiguntur quae in se culpam commerent,
plures uiri sint uidui quam nunc mulieres.—

ACTVS V

CHARINVS   V.i

CH. Limen superum<que> inferumque, salue, simul autem
                                             uale: 830
hunc hodie postremum extollo mea domo patria pedem.
usus, fructus, uictus, cultus iam mihi harunc aedium
interemptust, interfectust, alienatust. occidi!
di penates meum parentum, familiai Lar pater,
uobis mando, meum parentum rem bene ut tutemini. 835
ego mihi alios deos penatis persequar, alium Larem,
aliam urbem, aliam ciuitatem: ab Atticis abhorreo;
nam ubi mores deteriores increbrescunt in dies,
ubi qui amici, qui infideles sint nequeas pernoscere
ubique id eripiatur, animo tuo quod placeat maxume, 840
ibi quidem si regnum detur, non cupitast ciuitas.

EVTYCHVS CHARINVS   V.ii

EV. Diuom atque hominum quae spectatrix atque era eadem
                                           es hominibus,
spem speratam quom obtulisti hanc mihi, <tibi> gratis ago.
ecquisnam deus est, qui mea nunc laetus laetitia fuat?
domi erat quod quaeritabam: sex sodalis repperi, 845
uitam, amicitiam, ciuitatem, laetitiam, ludum, iocum;
eorum inuentu res simitu pessumas pessum dedi,
iram, inimicitiam, maerorem, lacrumas, exilium, inopiam
solitudinem, stultitiam, exitium, pertinaciam.
. . . .
date, di, quaeso conueniundi mi eius celerem copiam. 850
CH. apparatus sum ut uidetis: abicio superbiam;

egomet mihi comes, calator, equos, agaso, | armiger,
egomet sum mihi imperator, idem egomet mihi oboedio,
egomet mihi fero quod usust. o Cupido, quantus es!
nam tu quemuis confidentem facile tuis factis facis,   855
eundem ex confidente actutum diffidentem denuo.
EV. cogito quonam ego illum curram quaeritatum.
                                                    CH. certa res
me usque quaerere illam, quoquo | hinc abductast gentium;
neque mihi ulla opsistet amnis nec mons neque adeo mare,
nec calor nec frigus metuo neque uentum neque grandinem;
imbrem perpetiar, laborem sufferam, solem, sitim;   861
non concedam neque quiescam | usquam noctu neque dius
priu' profecto quam aut amicam aut mortem inuestigauero.
EV. nescioquoia uox ad auris mi aduolauit. CH. inuoco
uos, Lares uiales, ut me bene tutetis. EV. Iuppiter!   865
estne illic Charinus? CH. ciues, bene ualete. | EV. ilico
sta, Charine. CH. qui me reuocat? EV. Spes, Salus, Victoria.
CH. quid me uoltis? EV. ire tecum. | CH. alium comitem
                                            · quaerite,
non amittunt hi me comites qui tenent. EV. qui sunt ei?
CH. cura, miseria, aegritudo, lacrumae, lamentatio.   870
EV. repudia istos comites atque hoc respice et reuortere.
CH. siquidem mecum fabulari uis, supsequere. EV. sta ilico.
†sta ilico†, <nam> amicus <amico> aduenio multum
                                            beneuolens.   887
CH. male facis, properantem qui me commorare. sol abit. 873
EV. si huc item properes ut istuc properas, facias rectius:
huc secundus uentus nunc est; cape modo uorsoriam: 875
hic fauonius serenust, istic auster imbricus;
hic facit tranquillitatem, iste omnis fluctus conciet.
recipe te ad terram, Charine, huc. nonne ex aduorso uides,
nubis atra imberque <ut> instat? aspice ad sinisteram,
caelum ut est splendore plenum atque ut dei is<tuc uorti
                                            iubent>.   880
CH. religionem illic <mi> obiecit: recipiam me illuc.
                                            EV. sapis.
o Charine, contra pariter fer gradum et confer pedem,
porge bracchium. CH. prehende. iam tenes? EV. teneo.

CH. tene.
EV. quo nunc ibas? CH. exsulatum. EV. quid ibi faceres?
CH. quod miser.
EV. st!
ne paue, restituam iam ego te in gaudio antiquo ut sies. 885
maxume quod uis audire, id audies, quod gaudeas. 886
tuam amicam— CH. quid eam? EV. ubi sit ego scio.
CH. tune, opsecro? 888
EV. sanam et saluam. | CH. ubi eam saluam?
EV. ego scio. CH. ego me mauelim.
EV. potin ut animo sis tranquillo? CH. quid si mi animus
fluctuat? 890
EV. ego istum in tranquillo quieto tuto sistam: ne time.
CH. opsecro te, loquere <propere> | ubi sit, ubi eam uideris.
quid taces? dic. enicas me miserum tua reticentia.
EV. non longe hinc abest a nobis. CH. quin commostras, sei
uides?
EV. non uideo hercle nunc, sed uidi modo. CH. quin ego
uideam facis? 895
EV. faciam, CH. longum istuc amantist. EV. etiam metuis?
omnia
commonstrabo. amicior mihi nullus uiuit atque is est
qui illam habet, neque est quoi magi' me melius uelle aequom
siet.
CH. non curo istunc, de illa quaero. EV. de illa ergo ego dico
tibi. 899
sane hoc non in mentem uenit dudum, ut ubi <sit dicerem>.
CH. dic igitur, ubi illa est? EV. in nostris aedibus. CH. Aedis
probas,
si tu uera dicis, pulchre | aedificatas arbitro.
sed quid ego istuc credam? uidisti an de audito nuntias?
EV. egomet uidi. CH. quis eam adduxit ad uos? inque.
EV. <tu> rogas? 904
CH. uera dicis. EV. nil, Charine, te quidem quicquam pudet;
quid tua refert qui cum istac uenerit? CH. dum istic siet.
EV. est profecto. CH. opta ergo ob istunc nuntium quid uis
tibi.
EV. quid si optabo? CH. deos orato ut eius faciant copiam.
EV. derides. CH. seruata res est demum, si illam uidero. 909

sed quin ornatum hunc reicio? heus! aliquis actutum huc foras
exite illinc, pallium mi ecferte. EV. em, nunc tu mihi places.
CH. optume aduenis, puere, cape chlamydem atque istic sta
    ilico,
ut, si haec non sint uera, inceptum hoc itiner perficere
    exsequar.
EV. non mihi credis? CH. omnia equidem credo quae dicis
    mihi.
sed quin intro ducis me ad eam, ut uideam? EV. paullisper
    mane. 915
CH. quid manebo? EV. tempus non est intro eundi. |
    CH. enicas.
EV. non opus est, inquam, nunc intro te ire. CH. Responde
    mihi,
qua caussa? EV. operae non est. CH. qur? EV. quia non est
    illi commodum.
CH. itane? commodum illi non est, quae me amat, quam ego
    contra amo?
omnibus hic ludificatur me modis. ego·stultior,   920
qui isti credam. commoratur. chlamydem sumam denuo.
EV. mane parumper atque haec audi. CH. cape sis, puere, hoc
    pallium.
EV. mater irata est patri uehementer, quia scortum sibi
ob oculos adduxerit in aedis, dum ruri ipsa abest:
suspicatur illam amicam esse illi. CH. zonam sustuli.   925
EV. eam rem nunc exquirit intus. CH. iam machaerast in
    manu.
EV. nam si eo ted intro ducam— CH. tollo ampullam atque
    hinc eo.
EV. mane, mane, Charine. | CH. erras, <sic> me decipere
    hau potes.
EV. neque edepol uolo. CH. quin tu ergo itiner exsequi meum
    me sinis?
EV. non sino. CH. egomet me moror. tu puere, abi hinc intro
    ocius. 930
iam in currum escendi, iam lora | in manus cepi meas.
EV. sanus non es. CH quin, pedes, uos in curriculum conicitis
in Cyprum recta, quandoquidem pater mihi exsilium parat?

EV. stultus es, noli istuc quaeso dicere. CH. certum exsequist,
operam ut sumam ad peruestigandum ubi sit illaec. EV. quin
                                                       domist. 935
CH. nam hic quod dixit id mentitust. EV. uera dixi equidem
                                                            tibi.
CH. iam Cyprum ueni. EV. quin sequere, ut illam uideas
                                                      quam expetis.
CH. percontatus non inueni. EV. matris iam iram neglego.
CH. porro proficiscor quaesitum. nunc perueni Chalcidem;
uideo ibi hospitem Zacyntho, dico quid eo aduenerim,   940
rogito quis eam uexerit, quis habeat si ibi indaudiuerit.
EV. quin tu istas omittis nugas ac mecum huc intro ambulas?
CH. hospes respondit, Zacynthi ficos fieri non malas.
EV. nil mentitust. CH. sed de amica se indaudiuisse autumat,
hic Athenis esse. EV. Calchas iste quidem Zacynthiust.   945
CH. nauem conscendo, proficiscor ilico. iam sum domi,
iam redii <ex> exsilio. salue, mi sodalis Eutyche:
ut ualuisti? quid parentes mei? ualent mater pater?
bene uocas, benigne dicis: cras apud te, nunc domi.
sic decet, sic fieri oportet. EV. heia! quae mi somnias.   950
hic homo non sanust. CH. medicari amicus quin properas
                                                          <mihi>?
EV. sequere sis. CH. sequor. EV. clementer quaeso, calces
                                                          deteris.
audin tu? CH. iam dudum audiui. EV. pacem componi uolo
meo patri cum matre: nam nunc est irata | — CH. i modo. 954
EV. propter istanc. CH. i modo. EV. ergo cura. CH. quin tu
                                                         ergo i modo.
tam propitiam reddam, quam quom propitiast Iuno Ioui.

DEMIPHO LYSIMACHVS   V.iii

DE. Quasi tu numquam quicquam adsimile | huiius facti
                                                          feceris.
LY. edepol numquam; caui ne quid facerem. uix uiuo miser.
nam mea uxor propter illam tota in fermento iacet.
DE. at ego expurigationem habebo, ut ne suscenseat.   960
LY. sequere me. sed exeuntem filium uideo meum.

Plautus *Mercator*

EVTYCHVS LYSIMACHVS DEMIPHO V.iv

EV. Ad patrem ibo, ut matris iram sibi esse sedatam sciat.
iam redeo. LY. placet principium. quid agis? quid fit,
                                           Eutyche?
EV. optuma opportunitate ambo aduenistis. LY. quid rei est?
EV. uxor tibi placida et placatast. cette dextras nunciam. 965
LY. di me seruant. EV. tibi amicam | esse nullam nuntio.
DE. di te perdant! quid negotist nam, quaeso, istuc?
                                           EV. eloquar.
animum aduortite igitur ambo. DE. quin tibi ambo operam
                                           damus.
EV. qui bono sunt genere nati, <si> sunt ingenio malo,
suapte culpa degeneres fiiunt, genus ingenio inprobant. 970
DE. uerum hic dicit. LY. tibi ergo dicit. EV. eo illud est
                                           uerum magis.
nam te istac aetate haud aequom filio fuerat tuo
adulescenti amanti amicam eripere emptam argento suo.
DE quid tu ais? Charini amicast illa? EV ut dissimulat malus!
DE. ille quidem illam sese ancillam matri emisse dixerat. 975
EV. propterea igitur tu mercatu's, nouos amator, uetu' puer?
LY. optume hercle, perge, | ego adsistam hinc alterinsecus.
quibus est dictis dignus usque oneremus ambo. DE. Nullus
                                           sum.
LY. filio suo qui | innocenti fecit tantam iniuriam.
EV. quem quidem hercle ego, in exsilium quom | iret,
                                           redduxi domum; 980
nam ibat exsulatum. DE. an abiit? LY. etiam loquere, larua?
temperare istac aetate istis decet ted artibus.
DE. fateor, deliqui profecto. | EV. etiam loquere, larua?
itidem ut tempus anni, aetate alia aliud factum conuenit;
nam si istuc ius est, senecta aetate scortari senes, 985
ubi locist res summa nostra puplica? DE. ei, perii miser!
LY. adulescentes rei agendae isti magi' solent operam dare.
DE. iam opsecro hercle uobis habete cum porcis, cum fiscina.
EV. redde illi. DE. sibi habeat, iam ut uolt per me sibi habeat
                                           licet.
EV. temperi edepol, quoniam ut aliter facias non est copiae.
DE. supplici sibi sumat quid uolt ipse ob hanc iniuriam, 991

modo pacem faciatis oro, ut ne mihi iratus siet.
si hercle sciuissem siue adeo ioculo dixisset mihi
se illam amare, numquam facerem ut illam amanti
                            abducerem.
Eutyche, ted oro, sodalis eius es, serua et subueni: 995
hunc senem para clientem; memorem dices benefici.
LY. ora ut ignoscat delictis tuis atque adulescentiae.
DE. pergin tu autem? heia! superbe inuehere. spero ego mihi
                            quoque
tempus tale euenturum ut tibi gratiam referam parem.
LY. missas iam ego istas artis feci. DE. et quidem ego dehinc
                        iam. EV. nihil <agis>: 1000
consuetudine animus rusus te huc inducet. DE. opsecro,
sati' iam ut habeatis. quin loris caedite etiam, si lubet.
LY. recte dicis. sed istuc uxor faciet, quom hoc resciuerit.
DE. nihil opust resciscat. EV. quid istic? non resciscet, ne
                        time.
eamus intro, non utibilest hic locus, factis tuis,   1005
dum memoramus, arbitri ut sint qui praetereant per uias.
DE. hercle qui tu recte dicis: eadem breuior fabula
erit. eamus. EV. hic est intus filius apud nos tuos.
DE. optumest. illac per hortum nos domum transibimus.
LY. Eutyche, hanc uolo priu' rem agi, quam meum intro
                        refero pedem. 1010
EV. quid istuc est? LY. suam quisque homo rem meminit.
                        responde mihi:
certon scis non suscensere mihi tuam matrem? EV. scio.
LY. uide. EV. mea fide. LY. satis habeo. id quaeso hercle,
                        etiam uide.
EV. non mihi credis? LY. immo credo, sed tamen metuo
                        miser. 1014
DE. eamus intro. EV. immo dicamus senibus legem censeo,
priu' quam abeamus, qua se lege teneant contentique sint.
annos gnatus sexaginta qui | erit, si quem scibimus
si maritum siue hercle adeo caelibem scortarier,
cum eo nos hic lege agemus: inscitum arbitrabimur,
et per nos quidem hercle egebit qui suom prodegerit.   1020
neu quisquam posthac prohibeto | adulescentem filium

quin amet et scortum ducat, quod bono fiat modo;
siquis prohibuerit, plus perdet clam <qua>si praehibuerit
                                                        palam.
haec adeo | uti ex hac nocte primum lex teneat senes.   1024
bene ualete; atque, adulescentes, haec si uobis lex placet,
ob senum hercle industriam uos aequom est clare plaudere.

COMMENTARY

Abbreviations
< = "from"
cf. = "compare"
i.e. = "that is" (*id est*)
sc. = "supply, add" (*scilicet*)
OLD = *Oxford Latin Dictionary*
AG = *Allen and Greenough's New Latin Grammar*
Bennett = Bennett, C. E. 1910-1914. *Syntax of Early Latin* (vol. 1 and 2). Boston [reprint Hildesheim 1966]
Enk = P.J. Enk, 1932. *Plauti Mercator (cum prolegomenis, notis criticis, commentario exegetico)*. Leiden [reprint Arno Press 1979]
Lindsay, *Syntax* = Lindsay, W. M. 1907. *The Syntax of Plautus*. Oxford.

ARGUMENTUM I
Notice the acrostic with the title of the comedy. Such plot summaries were composed for many of the plays, probably in the second century CE.
Meter: iambic senarii (with free use of hiatus). See Introduction, Meter Cb 1.1.

$$- - | - \ \neg \ \smile \quad - | \smile \quad \smile \neg - \ - | \smile \ -$$
missus mercatum // ab su(o) adulescens patre

1   **mercatum** (< *mercor*): "trade, become a merchant"; supine of purpose (AG 509). After *mercatum*, there is hiatus (no elision of the ultima *–um*, before a vowel) at the *caesura*. Hiatus is marked in the text by |.
2   **emit** < *emo*, "buy."
    scita forma: "of fine appearance," i.e., "good looking"; ablative of description (AG 415a).
3   **requirit** < *requiro*, "ask, inquire." The subject is *senex*.
    quae sit: indirect question, depending on *requirit* (AG 573f).
4   **confingit** < *confingo*, "make up a story."
    emptam: sc. *esse*. The infinitive *esse* is implied. It is frequently omitted from future active and passive and from perfect passive infinitives.

4	**seruos**= *seruus*, i.e., of the young man.
	pedisequam: "female attendant."
6	**tradit** < *trado*, "deliver."
	uicino eum: There is hiatus at the *caesura* after *uicino*; *eum* is scanned as one syllable by synizesis (the running together of two syllables into one).
7	**obduxe**: syncopated form of *obduxisse*, < *obduco*, "bring over."
	scortum: "prostitute."
	Charinum: the son of the old man Demipho. There is hiatus after *Charinum*.
8	**sodalis**: "companion, friend"; hiatus after *amicam*.

ARGUMENTUM II
Non-acrostic summary of the play, probably added around the fifth century CE.
Meter: iambic senarii (with free use of hiatus). See Introduction, Meter Cb 1.1.

$$\bar{\ }\ \rceil\quad \breve{\ }\ \rceil\bar{\ }\quad \rceil\breve{\ }\quad \bar{\ }\mid \bar{\ }\ \bar{\ }\mid\breve{\ }\ \bar{\ }$$
mèrcat(um) asotum // fili(um) extrudit pater

1	**asotum**: "prodigal."
	extrudit < *extrudo*, "expel."
2	**peregre**: "abroad."
3	**exilit** < *ex(s)ilio*, "jump out."
4	**aduolat** < *aduolo*, "fly towards, hasten."
	deperit < *depereo*, "be desperately in love with"; + an accusative object, *ancillam*. There is hiatus after *uisam*.
5	**cuius sit**: " whose she is"; indirect question, depending on *percontatur* (< *percontor*, "ask").
6	**<ait>**: Angle brackets are used to indicate the addition of a word not present in the manuscript. The bracketed words are necessary to complete the sentence.
	ipsius: "his"; genitive of possession.
7	**prospiciens** < *prospicio*, "look out for"; + dative (AG 370).
8	**ueniret**: "that she be sold"; subjunctive in the jussive clause (substantive clause of purpose) after *orabat* (AG 563).
	ueniret < *ueneo*= *uenum ire*, "go to sale"; used as the passive of *uendo* (= *uenum do*, "give for sale, sell").

Plautus *Mercator*

       natus ut suo: sc. *natus orabat patrem ut ancilla ueniret suo amico.*
9   **hic filium subdiderat uicini**: "he (i.e., Charinus) had appointed the son of the neighbor in his place"; *subdiderat < subdo, OLD subdo* 7.
10   **praemercatur**: "buys first."
11   **domi**: "at home"; locative.
12   **insimulat**: "accuses"; with predicate accusative *scortum* (AG 392).
       protelat < *protelo*, "rout (with a verbal attack)."
13   **expes**: "hopeless."
15   **suopte**: The suffix *–pte* intensifies the possessive adjective.

ACT I, SCENE i
On stage you can see a street in Athens and two houses, that of Demipho and that of Lysimachus. Entrance or exit from the left leads to the harbor, from the right to the city (*agora, forum*). Charinus gives the audience all the information they need about his father and his love affairs in Athens and in Rhodes.
Meter: Iambic Senarii. See Introduction, Meter Cb 1.1.

      ¯   ¯ | ˘ ¯ | ¯   ˘ ˘|˘ ¯| ¯ ¯ | ˘ ¯
          duas res simul nunc // agere decretumst mihi

1   **duas**: scanned as one syllable by synizesis.
       decretumst mihi (< *decerno*): "it has been decided by me," i.e., "I have decided." The infinitive *agere* is the subject of this impersonal expression (AG 454-455). See Introduction, Meter Ca 2 on prodelision (*decretum est*).
2   **eloquar** < *eloquor*, "divulge, reveal, explain."
3   **item ... ut**: "just as, likewise."
4   **<ui>** < *uis*, "force, power"; ablative of manner or cause (AG 412b and 404).
       Dii: dative; archaic form of *diei*. The Day, the Night, the Sun, and the Moon are all personified gods, to whom lovers, according to Charinus, address their prayers.
5   **Soli** (< *sol*): "sun."
6   **quos**: The relative pronoun acts as a connective (*OLD qui*[1] 14; AG 308f), in this case equivalent to *eos*.

Plautus *Mercator*

6   **pol**: "by Pollux!"; also found as *edepol* (127). Pollux and his twin brother Castor (the *Dioskouroi*, "sons of Zeus") are frequently invoked in comedy. Both men and women call on Pollux, but only women on Castor.
    credo: There is hiatus before *humanas*.
    querimonias: "complaints."

7   **non tanti facere**: "do not greatly value"; *tanti* is a genitive of value (AG 417).
    quid uelint: indirect question, depending on *non tanti facere*.

8   **meas**: one syllable by synizesis.

9   **Graece**: adverb, "in Greek." In the next line, we see *Latine*, "in Latin."
    haec: sc. *fabula*, "this play."
    Emporos: "Merchant"; for Philemon and his play see the Introduction A.

10   **Macci Titi**: See the Introduction A for details about Plautus' name.

11   **mercatum** (< *mercatus*): "trade." Given the active trade between Athens and Rhodes, it is natural for the playwright to choose it as Charinus' destination. For Athens' trade with its colonies see J. Boardman, *The Greeks Overseas* (London 1964).
    hinc: "from here."
    Rhodum: "to Rhodes." In classical Latin, the accusative of *place to which* and the ablative of *place from which* do not need a preposition with the names of towns and small islands, or with *domus* and *rus* (AG 427).

12   **abii** < *abeo*, "leave."
    domo: "from my house"; ablative of *place from which* (see on 11).

13   **occepi** < *occipio*, "begin."
    forma eximia: "of extraordinary beauty"; ablative of description (see on Argumentum I 2).

14   **ea**: sc. *muliere*.
    implicitus= *implicatus* < *implico*, "involve intimately" (*OLD implico* 6-7). *ut* ("how") introduces an indirect question (see on Argumentum I 3).
    si operaest auribus: "if you have some free time to listen," literally, "if your ears have some free time" (< *operae est*,

Plautus *Mercator*

    "there is free time, leisure"); *operae* is a genitive of value with *est* and a possessive dative (Bennett 2.96).

15 **aduortendum ad animum**: "to pay attention," literally, "to turn your mind"; the preposition, as often, appears in the middle of its phrase. The gerundive expresses purpose (AG 506).
    benignitas: "kindness."

16 **et hoc**: "this too"; i.e., his involvement with the girl.
    parum: "not at all."
    hercle: "by Hercules!" This is another frequent interjection in comedy, but Hercules is called upon only by men.
    more: "according to the custom" (AG 412).
    institi < *insisto*, "apply oneself; pursue vigorously."

17 The daggers indicate that the line is hopelessly corrupt in the manuscript— what editors call a *locus desperatus*.

18 **sectari** < *sector*, "accompany."

19 **aegritudo**: "distress, sickness."
    elegantia: "refinement." Refinement and taste are considered not manly virtues but rather attributes of àn effeminate person.

20 **haec**: specifically refers to *elegantia* in 19 but also includes *cura* and *aegritudo*.
    quemque= *quemcumque*, "whomsoever."
    attigit < *attingo*, "come in contact with"; the subject is *haec*.

    ‒   ‒ | ˘   ‒ | ‒   ˘ ˘ | ‒   ‒ | ‒   ‒ | ˘ ‒
    haec non mod(o) illum qui amat sed quemqu(e) attigit
    [Note: *qui* is shortened by prosodic hiatus. See Introduction, Meter Ca 4d.]

21 **multat** < *multo*, "punish."

22 **profecto**: "assuredly."

23 **praequam res patitur**: "beyond what his fortune (*res*) allows," i.e., "beyond his means."
    studuit < *studeo*, "be eager for"; + dative (AG 367).

24 **minus**: "not."

25 **aerumna**: "hardship, tribulation."

26 **ineptia**: nominative, but scan as *ĭnēptĭā*; the syllable is lengthened before *st-* in the following word. See Introduction, Meter Ca 1.
    adeo: "to such a degree; to such an extent."

26	**temeritas**: "thoughtlessness."
27	**excors**: "silly."
28	**petulantia**: "wantonness."
29	**desidia**: "sloth."
30	**inopia**: "helplessness."
	dispendium: "expense, loss."
31	**ideo ... quia**: "for this reason ... because." The redundancy is common in classical Latin also. See Introduction, Meter Cb 1.1 for scansion.
32	**quae nihil attingunt ad rem**: "which are irrelevant to the situation"; the relative clause is the object of *profert* (33).
	usui: "useful"; dative of purpose (AG 382.1).
33	**tam**= *tamen* (*OLD tam* 7).
	profert < *profero*, "express."
	aduorso < *aduersus*, "unfavorable; wrong."
34	**hoc**: modifies *multiloquium* of 31.
	hoc pauciloquium ... praedico: "I declare this over-talking (*multiloquium*) under-talking"; predicate accusative to *hoc* after *praedico* (AG 393). *pauciloquium* is a variation of *parumloquium* of 31; *praedico* < *praedico*, "pronounce; declare."
34-35	**rusum Idcirco ... / quia**. "again for that reason ... because" (*rusum*= *rursum*).
35	**callide**: "artfully."
36	**quae in rem sint suam**: "the things which are to his own advantage"; this relative clause is the object of the infinitive *loqui* and has the verb in the subjunctive mood, by attraction to the subjunctive *possit* in the *ut* result clause (AG 593 and Bennett 1.305f).
37	**mi**= *mihi*.
38	**eodem**: modifies *die*; *eo-* is pronounced as a single syllable by synizesis.
	Venu': See Introduction, Meter Ca 1 for the elision of the final *s*.
	legauit < *lego*, "appoint; bequeath"; understand the verb with both clauses. The verb is used as if Charinus inherited love and longwindedness from Venus, just as a son inherits property from his parents.
39	**illuc**: "to this point."

reuorti < *reuertor*, "return."
conata (< *conor*): "what I have tried" (literally, "the things attempted," i.e., with regard to the love affair).

40 **<ut ex> ephebis aetate exii**: "when I departed from the ephebes in age," i.e., "when I came of age." For this idiomatic use of the preposition see AG 221.11c. The conjunction *ut*, as often, introduces a temporal clause and takes the perfect indicative (AG 543). An *ephebus* is an adolescent.

42 **coepi**: "began" (AG 205).
hinc: "from this point."
ilico: "on that very spot; immediately."

43 **res**: "property."
exsulatum: "into exile"; supine of purpose (AG 509). The expression is figurative for Charinus' squandering of his father's property on the *meretrix*.
clam ... patris: "unknown to my father"; this adverb is followed by genitive or accusative (AG 432d). Scan as *clăm ăbībāt*, since *clam* is shortened in prosodic hiątus (see on 20).

44 **leno**: "pimp."

45 **ut quidque poterat rapiebat domum**: "he was pillaging my house, whatever he was able to plunder"; here the correlative conjunction *ut* means "as" (AG 323g).

46 **obiurigare** (< *obiurgo*, archaic *obiurigo*): "he reprimanded"; historical infinitive (AG 463). The infinitive is often used for the imperfect indicative in lively narration.

47 **expromere** (< *expromo*, OLD *expromo* 3): "he revealed"; historical infinitive.

48 **suam**: treated as one syllable by synizesis.
illius: sc. *lenonis*; scan as bisyllabic, *īllī(u)s*.
augerier= *augeri*; archaic passive infinitive < *augeo*, "increase."

49 **mussans** < *musso*, "speak in a low voice; grumble."

49-52 A series of historical infinitives (see on 46): *conloqui, abnuere, negitare, conclamitare, praedicere*.

50 **adeo**: "even the fact that."

51 **praedicere** < *praedico*, "admonish, warn"; introduces a jussive clause (substantive clause of purpose) with *ut*, as often, omitted (AG 565).

53

52 **tenerent**= *abstinerent*, "they should refrain from"; + infinitive (AG 558b).
    mutuitanti < *mutuo*, "borrow money." The participle is in the dative, governed by the infinitive *credere*.
53 **inlexe**: syncopated for *inlexisse* < *illicio*, "lure, entice." Charinus is reporting his father's words in indirect statement; the infinitives used through 78 depend on the verbs of saying from the previous sentence in 51, *conclamitare* and *praedicere*.
    dispendium: See on 30.
54 **intemperantem, non modestum**: governed by *me* in the next line.
    iniurium: sc. *esse*, "[he said] that I was unjust, wrongful."
55 **trahere, exhaurire**: The two infinitives are in an asyndeton, i.e., the conjunction that would have connected them is omitted (AG 640).
    quirem < *queo*, "be able" (for the defective verb *queo* and its opposite, *nequeo*, see AG 206d). The relative clauses *quod quirem* and *quae inuenisset* (56-57) have verbs in the subjunctive since they are subordinate clauses in indirect discourse (AG 579f).
    ab se domo: *a sua domo*.
56 **ratione pessuma**: "by the worst conduct."
    ipsus= *ipse*.
    ea ... optuma: accusative subject of the infinitives *diffunditari* and *didier* in 58.
57 **omnis labores**: object of *perferens*.
    inuenisset < *inuenio*, "acquire, earn."
58 **diffunditari** < *diffundito*, "spend frequently."
    didier= *didi* < *dido*, "scatter."
59 **conuicium ... me ... se pascere**: "[he said that] he was feeding me (to become) a disgrace"; *conuicium* is a predicate accusative to *me* (AG 393).
60 **quod nisi puderet, ne luberet uiuere**: "if I were not ashamed of this, I should not wish to live"; in direct discourse, the father says: *nisi te pudeat, ne libeat tibi uiuere*. *ne* is used as the negative in hortatory subjunctive (AG 439); for the syntax of the impersonal *pudet* see AG 354b.

61	**extemplo ... postquam**: "as soon as." The clause is in the subjunctive since it is a subordinate temporal clause in indirect discourse (see on 55).
63	**operam dedisse** < *operam do*, "give one's attention, apply one's efforts."
	sibi: dative of possession (AG 373).
64	**arte**: "strictly."
	cohibitum < *cohibeo*, "restrict."
65	**opere** < *opus*, "work, job."
	inmundo <*inmundus*, "dirty." Living as a farmer was considered by the Romans a blessing, the epitome of virtue and morality.
	exercitum < *exerceo*, "train."
66	**quinto anno quoque**: "within the period of five years, every five years"; ablative of time within which (AG 424). *quoque* < *quisque*, "every, each."
	solitum < soleo, "be accustomed"; sc. *esse*.
67	**ut spectauisset peplum**: *ut* introduces a subordinate temporal clause (see on 40), followed by a pluperfect subjunctive in indirect speech (AG 543). The festival of the Panathenaea in honor of Athena, the virgin goddess, culminated with the procession of a new robe (*peplum*) to her statue in the Parthenon.
68	**rus**: accusative of place to which; see on 11 (AG 427). Notice the alliteration: *rus rusum*.
	confestim: "immediately."
	exigi < *exigo*, "require, force."
69	**multo**: "by far"; ablative of degree of difference (AG 414).
	primum ... familiarium: "first among the household slaves."
70	**quom**= *cum*; see Introduction, Language B 3b. It is elided here.
71	**tibi**: "for yourself"; dative of reference (AG 376). The line has a proverbial ring.
	aras < *aro*, "plough."
	occas < *occo*, "harrow."
	seris < *sero*, "sow."
	idem: "you yourself, at the same time"; emphatic use of the pronoun.

71	**metis** < *meto*, "reap."
72	**pariet** < *pario*, "give birth, bear."
	labos= *labor*.
73	**recesset**: syncopated for *recessiset* < *recedo*, "depart"; subjunctive in a subordinate clause in indirect discourse.
74	**uendidisse** < *uendo*, "sell."
	ea pecunia: ablative of means.
75	**metreta**: about 9 gallons; a ship of 2700 gallons was considered very large.
	quae... tolleret: "which could take a weight of"; relative clause of purpose (AG 531.2).
76	**parasse**= syncopated form of *parauisse* < *paro*, "prepare, acquire."
	ea (sc. *naue, naui*): ablative of means.
	mercis < *merx*, "merchandise."
	uectatum (< *uecto*): "(pass.) ride, drive, travel" (*OLD vecto* 2); sc. *esse*.
77	**adeo dum**: "to the point until" (*OLD adeo* 2); *peperisset* < *pario* (see on 72).
78	**me idem decere, si ut deceret me forem**: "[he said that] this very same thing would befit me, if I were as it is fitting for me." The protasis of the contrary-to-fact present conditional *si forem* (*forem*= *essem*) has an apodosis in the indirect statement infinitive *decere* (in direct discourse, *deceret*). Charinus' father brings up the example of his own youth in order to teach his son good morals. As often, Plautus touches on the issue of the gap between the generations.
79-80	The line appears as one line in the manuscripts and is traditionally numbered likewise. Scan *ego* with iambic shortening on the ultima (see Introduction, Meter Ca 4b) and *meo* as one syllable by synizesis.
	ubi: "when"; temporal clause (AG 543).
81	**odio me esse quoi**: "that I am hated (by the one) to whom." Understand *ei* as antecedent to *quoi* (= *cui*; see Introduction, Language B 3b), dative after *placere*.
	aequom fuit: "it was right."
82	**amens amans**: Notice the word play.
	animum offirmo meum: "I make up my mind (on a course of action)."

83	**mercatum**: See on Argumentum I 1.
84	**amorem missum facere me**: "put my love aside"; *missum facio*, "discharge, dismiss from service" (*OLD mitto* 3b). Love is often linked to military service (the so-called *militia amoris*).
	dum illi opsequar: "provided that I obey him"; subjunctive in a proviso clause (AG 528).
85	Scan: *ăgĭt* (iambic shortening) *grātiās*.
86	**persequi** (< *persequor*): "to follow up."
87	**cercurum**: a long boat of Asian origin.
88	**parata naui**: ablative absolute.
89	**talentum**: a Greek unit of value, consisting of sixty *mnae* (or *minae*). It was a very significant amount of money.
90	**una**: "together with me, at the same time" (adverb).
91	**paedagogus**: a private teacher assigned to wealthy boys.
	uti= *ut*.
92	**his confectis**: ablative absolute; *confectis* < *conficio*, "complete, accomplish."
	nauim soluimus: "we weigh anchor."
94	**ex sententia**: "in my opinion; as I thought best."
95	**lucrum ingens**: "huge profit."
	praeterquam: "over and beyond."
	meu': For the elision of the final *s* see 38.
96	**aestumatas**= *aestimatas*, "valued"; *quas* is implied for the sentence *meu' pater dedit*.
	peculium: "private property; pocket money."
97	**illi**: adverbial locative, equivalent of *illic*, "there, at that place."
99	**decumbo**: "recline"; a usual description of dining, since the Romans used to recline on couches to eat.
	hilare: "cheerfully."
	ampliter: for *ample*, "splendidly."
100	**discubitum** (< *discumbo*): "to sleep"; supine of purpose after *imus* (AG 509).
	noctu: "at night" (adverbial ablative).
	ut imus: temporal *ut*, here with a historical present.
101	**qua**: ablative of comparison after *pulchrior* (AG 406-407).
102	**iussu**: "by the order of."

103 **uosmet**: The suffix *–met* is attached to the personal pronoun for emphasis.
quam: "how"; introduces an indirect question.
104 **postridie**: "the following day."
adeo: "I approach."
105 **eius pro meritis**: "for his services"; the noun modified by *eius* is *hospitem* in 104.
munem (< *munis, -is, -e*): "obliged."
fore: future infinitive of *sum*.
106 **quid uerbis opus est**: "what need is there for words?"; *opus est* + ablative (AG 411).
aduexi < *adueho*, "bring, transport, carry to."; there is hiatus after *emi* at the *caesura* of the fourth foot.
107 **eam**: synizesis (also in 108).
resciscat < *rescisco*, "find out"; for the omission of *ut* see on 51.
108 **modo**: "just now."
109 **conspicor**: "I see."
110 **uetui** < *ueto*, "forbid."
timeo quid siet: "I fear what this may be"; *quid siet* is indirect question (*siet = sit*, see Introduction B 2f).

ACT I, SCENE ii
In this scene Acanthio the slave is introduced. He is a typical *seruus currens*, a stock character in Roman comedy. The slave enters at a run (*currens*), full of news and worried about his master's troubles. Meter: 111-116; 118-128; 132-133; 137-140: Iambic Octonarii (Intro Meter Cb 1.3)

```
 -  -  |  -  ˘ ˘| -   - | ˘ -  |        ˘       - | ˘  -| ˘ -| -
ex summis opibus uiribusqu(e) :: usqu(e) experire nitere
```

117; 129-131: Trochaic Septenarii (Intro Meter Cb 2.1)

```
 -  - | -  ˘ ˘| -       - |  -   - | -         -| -  -| - ˘ |-
currenti properant(i) hau quisquam :: dign(um) habet decedere
```

134: Iambic Senarius (Intro Meter Cb 1.1)

```
 -   -| ˘ - |-   ˘ ˘| -   - |  ˘ ˘       - | ˘  -
quae te malae res // agitant mult(ae) ere t(e) atque me
```

135-136: Iambic Dimeters (Intro Meter Cb 3.1 for scansion of 135)

141-224: Trochaic Septenarii (Intro Meter Cb 2.1)

```
 ˘ ˘    ˉ|   ˉˉ| ˉ  ˉ|ˉ   |   ˉ   ˉ|ˉ  ˉ| ˉ  ˉ|ˉ
homin(em) eg(o) iracundiorem :: quam te noui neminem
```

111 **ex summis opibus uiribusque**: "with the maximum of your resources and strength."
experire, nitere: second person singular present imperatives of the deponent verbs *experior*, "try, endure" and *nitor*, "endeavor."
usque: "constantly."

112 **erus ... minor**: "the younger master," i.e., Charinus.
seruetur < *seruo*, "preserve, save."
agedum: "come!"; a common exhortation in comedy.

113 **abige** < *abigo*, "drive off; expel."
aps te= *a te*.
lassitudinem: "exhaustion, fatigue."
caue pigritiae praeuorteris: "take care not to succumb to sloth," i.e., "don't give in to laziness"; *caue* is used in prohibitions with the perfect subjunctive in archaic Latin, as here (AG 450 and 450 n.3).
praeuorteris < *praeuerto*, "succumb"; + dative.

114 **enicat suspiritus**: "my breath exhausts me; I can hardly breathe; I am almost dead"; < *enico*, "kill."
suffero: "stand, endure."
anhelitum: "panting."

115 **plenis semitis qui aduorsum eunt**: "those who come opposite in the crowded streets." The verb *enicant* [*me*] is implied after this relative clause.
aspellito < *aspello*, "drive away"; second person singular future active imperative. For the use of future imperatives in Plautus see Introduction, Language B 2d.

116 **detrude** < *detrudo*, "push off"; sc. *de uia*.
deturba < *deturbo*, "throw down." There is hiatus after *in uiam* (*diaeresis*).
disciplina: "practice, habit."
hic: "here"; adverb (*OLD hic*²).

117 **hau**= *haud*, "not; hardly" (negative particle).

117   **dignum habet**: "considers it appropriate."
currenti properanti ... decedere: "to make way for (someone) running, hurrying"; *decedere* < *decedo*, "yield, make way for"; + dative. The two participles are in asyndeton.

118   **tres ... res agendae sunt**: "three things are to be done," "three things must be done." The future passive participle (*agendae*) expresses necessity or obligation. It is often, as here, combined with a form of *sum* in what is called the passive periphrastic conjugation. For examples see AG 196.
simitu= *simul*.
quando: "whenever"; + future perfect introduces a temporal indefinite clause that follows the syntax of conditionals (AG 542).
unam: Understand *rem*.
occeperis < *occipio*, "begin."

119   **currendum et pugnandum et ... iurigandum est**: "one must run and fight and brawl." The future passive participles of intransitive verbs must be used impersonally in the passive periphrastic (i.e., they must be in the neuter singular with a third person singular form of *sum*). See AG 500.3.

120   **quid illuc est quod ille ... exquirit cursuram**: "what is the reason that he tries to find an opportunity to run"; the relative pronoun *quod* functions as an accusative of the inner object in the expression *quid est quod*, "what is the reason that."
illuc= *illud + ce*. See Introduction, Language B 3c; scan as *ĭllūc* by iambic shortening caused by the accent on the ultimate syllable.
expedite: "quickly." Notice the alliteration *expedite exquirit*.

121   **curaest**: "it is of concern" (understand *mihi*); *curae* is a dative of purpose.
negoti quid: "what of business," i.e., "what business"; *negoti* is partitive genitive with *quid* (AG 346a1).
sit ... nuntiet: both subjunctives in indirect question.
nugas ago: "I accomplish nothing; it is of no use."

122   **quam ... tam**: "the more ... the more"; here used with the superlative *maxime* (*OLD quam* 5).
restito: frequentative form of *resto*, "linger."

> **res in periclo uortitur**: "the situation turns in danger; the situation becomes dangerous."

123   **mali nescioquid**: "something bad," literally, "something of evil"; *mali* is partitive genitive (see on 121). *nescioquid*: "something," literally, "I do not know what"; scan as *nēscĭŏquīd*.
     genua: "knees."
     cursorem: "runner"; *hunc* refers to Acanthio himself.

124   **perii**: "I am dead" (< *pereo*, "die, perish).
     seditionem facit lien: "my spleen stirs up a mutiny."
     occupat praecordia: "it takes hold of my vitals." The spleen is enlarged by disease, causing heart palpitations. It is here comically personified as a soldier, organizing a mutiny against the slave's will. See Introduction, Meter Cb 1.3 for scansion.

125   **animam nequeo uertere**: "I am unable to catch my breath."
     nimi' nihili tibicen siem: "I would be a very poor flute player"; *nihili* is a genitive of value (see on 7).

127   **balineae**: "baths."
     eximent < *eximo*, "remove."
     Scan as *mĭhĭ hănc lāssĭtūdĭn(em)* by iambic shortening of *hanc*.

126   **laciniam**: "the flap, hem of the cloak."
     apsterge < *abstergo*, "wipe."
     tibi: The dative of separation is common with verbs of taking away, such as *apsterge* here (AG 381).

128   **domin**= *domine*, "at home"; the vowel of the interrogative particle *–ne* is elided.
     foris: "outside, out"; locative (AG 427.3a).
     animi pendeo: "I am uncertain, in suspense"; *animi* is a locative or genitive of respect (AG 358).

129   **illuc**: Scan as *īllŭc* by iambic shortening caused by the accent on *quid*.
     †**ex hoc metu ut sim certus.**†: For the daggers see on 17; as it stands, the second part of the septenarius presents serious metrical problems.

130   **cesso**: frequentative form of *cedo*, "be inactive, hesitate"; + infinitive.

130 **foribus facere hisce assulas**: "to smash these doors into pieces," literally, "to make splinters to these doors."
131 **aperite aliquis**: "open it, somebody!" *aperite*: plural imperative < *aperio*, "open." A plural verb with a singular subject is common when one refers to a group of people (Lindsay, *Syntax* I.6).
132 **num**: anticipates a negative answer (AG 332b).
ostium: "door."
arbitratur < *arbitror*, "consider, think."
ecce me: Charinus has just come out of the house of his father Demipho.
133 **nusquamst disciplina ignauior**: "nowhere can you find slower service (i.e., than here)!" Acanthio is complaining about the behavior of the other house slaves who did not open the door immediately.
134 **multae te atque me**: sc. *res agitant*.
135 See Introduction, Meter Cb 3.1 for scansion.
135a **principium**: "prologue, introduction."
dato: second person singular future active imperative.
136 **at tibi sortito id optigit**: "but this befell you by lot." *optingo*, "fall as one's lot, occur to the (dis)advantage of"; + dative.
sortito < *sortior*, "obtain by lot."
137 **loquere**: second person singular present imperative of the deponent *loquor*.
placide: "calmly."
adquiescere < *adquiesco*, "rest."
138 **tua caussa**: "for your sake"; *caussa* is the archaic spelling of *causa* (AG 359b).
rupi ramites: "I burst my lungs."
iam dudum: "for some time now."
sputo: "I spit." Latin idiom uses a present tense with *iam dudum*, while English expects a present perfect, i.e., "I have been spitting" (AG 466).
139 **resinam ex melle**= "resin dipped in honey"; for the peculiar use of the preposition *ex* see *OLD ex* 19b. This product taken from trees was used as a type of bitter syrup.
uorato < *uoro*, "swallow"; second person singular future active imperative.

saluom feceris: sc. *te*, "you will make yourself healthy." The future perfect often replaces the simple future in early Latin by metrical convenience or to emphasize the instantaneous completion of the verb's action (Bennett 1.54-57).

140 **picem** < *pix*, "pitch."
bibito < *bibo*, "drink"; second person singular future active imperative.
apscesserit < *abscedo*, "disappear"; for the tense see on 139.

141 **iracundiorem** <*iracundus*, "hot-tempered."
quam te: "than you"; when *quam* is used in the comparison, both words are put in the same case, here in the accusative (*neminem iracundiorem ... quam te*). See AG 407.
noui: "I know"; < *nosco*, "become acquainted with."

142 **maledicentiorem** < *maledicens*, "abusive."

143 **sin**: used as a follow-up contrast to the preceding sentence.
sin id consuadeo, quod tibi saluti esse censeo: "but why [sc. Do you call me evil], if I persuade you to do what I think to be a cure for you?"
saluti < *salus*, "cure, well-being, salvation"; dative of purpose.

144 **apage**: "away with, get out!"; + accusative (here *salutem*).
istiusmodi: "of that kind"; the demonstrative of the second person *iste* ("that person or thing of yours or near you") is used here with contempt, as pejorative (AG 297c). Scan as *īstī(us)mŏdī*.
cruciatu < *cruciatus*, "torment."

145 **an boni quid usquamst**: "whether or not there is anything good anywhere"; double question introduced by *an*, depending on *dic* (AG 335b).
quod (sc. *bonum*) **quisquam uti possiet**: "which (good thing) any one could use (i.e., enjoy)." This is a relative clause of purpose (see on 75); *uti* < *utor* + accusative in archaic Latin (AG 410 n.1), *possiet= possit*.

146 **ne laborem capias**: "without your incurring trouble," literally, "on the understanding that you would not toil." *ne* serves here in a negative stipulative clause with the force of "without" and a verbal noun (Bennett 1.266). Charinus talks like a philosopher, pondering the existence of pure, good

happiness without the presence of evil woes, which make people toil in order to achieve their goal.

quom illo uti uoles: *cum* + future indicative in a temporal clause; *uti* used with an ablative (compare 145).

147 **didici** < *disco*, "learn."

148 **malum quo accedit**: "to which evil is added;" the antecedent of *quo* is *bonum*.

149 **cedo** (archaic imperative; pl. *cette*, see on 965): "give" (*OLD cedo*²). Scan: *cĕdŏ*.

em= *eme*, "take this!"; an interjection. Scan: *ĕm*.

150 **uin**= *uis ne*.

opsequentem < *obsequor*, "obey."

neuis= *non uis*.

opera: "by the fact, result" (adverbial ablative).

151 **experiri** < *experior*, "experience"; sc. *te* (subject).

currendo: "by running"; ablative of the gerund (AG 507).

152 **quae scirem**: subjunctive by attraction to *liceret* (see on 36).

actutum: "immediately."

153 **<cis>**: "within"; + accusative. Charinus promises Acanthio emancipation.

mensis= *mensès* < *mensis*, "month."

palpo percutis: "you beat me up with flatteries," literally, "you strike with the palm of your hand."

155 **ausim**= *ausus sim* < *audeo*, "dare." See Introduction, Language B 2g.

proloqui: "to utter"; complementary infinitive with *ausim*.

156 **quin**: "in fact."

sei= *si*.

mentiri < *mentior*, "lie."

ah: interjection expressing distress or strong objection.

157 **addunt** < *addo*, "inflict."

158 **sicine**: "in this way."

opsequens es: The present active participle is colloquially used with forms of *sum*, as is in English and the Romance languages (Lindsay, *Syntax* V.44).

159 **dice**= *dic*.

160 **dormientis**: accusative plural, alternative ending in *–is*, present active participle of *dormio*, "sleep," modifying

spectatores. Plautus is making fun of any members of the audience who have dozed off.
ne ... excites: "that you may wake up"; fear clause (AG 564).

161 **uae tibi**: "damn you," "go to hell!"
a portu adporto: Notice the alliteration.
162 **iurgium**: "altercation; quarrel."
163 **thensaurum ... mali**: Notice the oxymoron.
huc: "to this place" (adverb).
164 **immo**: "no; on the contrary"; contradicts the previous statement.
miserum: sc. *me esse*.
tacens < *taceo*, "keep silent."
165 **istuc**: Scan as *illuc* in 129 by iambic shortening; as often in Plautus, *istuc* is used here as a demonstrative of the second person that does not involve contempt (compare 144).
ne rogites: "don't keep asking!"; *ne* + subjunctive is often used to express a prohibition (AG 450 and 450 n.3). *rogito*, "ask repeatedly," is a frequentative of *rogo*.
166 **opsecro**: "I beg."
dissolue < *dissoluo*, "relieve" (sc. *timore*, "from fear").
animi pendeo: See on 128.
167 **priu' ... quam uapulem**: "before I may be flogged"; < *uapulo*, "be flogged" (passive in meaning). The tmesis (i.e., separation of the two parts of a compound word) of *priusquam* is also common in classical Latin; for the subjunctive after *priusquam* see AG 551c.
168 **uero**: "in truth, in fact."
loquere= *loqueris*; second person present indicative.
169 **sis**= *si uis*, "if you wish; please." Acanthio speaks aside, probably addressing the audience. Scan: *sīs*.
palpatur < *palpor*, "act in a soothing, cajoling manner"; *ut palpatur* is indirect question with the indicative, as often in early Latin (AG 575c).
occepit: See on 13.
171 **quandoquidem**: "since indeed; seeing that." Scan: *quāndŏquĭdēm*; the *o* in *quando* is shortened when it is joined with *quidem* by a process called *enclisis*.

171 **mihi supplicandum** (*esse*): "that supplication must be made to," "that I must be a suppliant to," "that I must beseech,"; + dative. *mihi* is a dative of agent (AG 374a) with the impersonal passive periphrastic construction of the intransitive *supplico* (see on 119).
meo: synizesis.
172 **tandem**: "now."
equidem: "indeed."
174 **armamenta**: "equipment of the ship; tackle."
quin expedis: "why don't you explain?"; < *expedio*, "make clear, explain."
175 **quid siet quod**: See on 120.
modo: See on 108.
176 **ex ore orationem mi eripis**: Notice the alliteration. *ex ore*: "from my mouth."
mi= *mihi*, dative of separation (see on 126).
177 **instes** < *insto*, "press on, urge forward." This is a future-less-vivid condition (AG 516).
acriter: "violently."
178 **flagitas** < *flagito*, "demand, keep asking."
179 **facias palam** < *facio palam*, "reveal."
180 **tuo'**= *tuus*. See Introduction, Language B 1b.
181 **tuam amicam**: Scan as *tŭăm ămīcām* (prosodic hiatus of *tuam*); *eam* is monosyllabic by synizesis.
183 **qui**= *quo*, "how"; see Introduction, Language B 3h.
quo pacto: "in what manner?"
hiantibus: "with them wide open"; ablative of means or manner. Because of the quick exchange of speakers, there is a hiatus after *uidere* and after *pacto*.
184 **in' hinc dierectus**: "go from here straight to hell!"; *in '*= *ini* < *ineo*.
nugare= *nugaris* < *nugor*, "talk nonsense"; second person singular present indicative.
in re capitali mea: "in this difficult situation when my life (*caput*) is at stake."

in hinc dierectus nugar(e):: in re capitali mea
185 **qui**: See on 183.
malum: "damn it; you evil!" (colloquial interjection).

186	Scan the monosyllabic *tam*, *quam*, and *te* with prosodic hiatus; for emphasis, they do not elide. There is also iambic shortening of the words preceding or following them (*hercle*, *certe*, *ego*).
187	**ut ... astitit**: "as he stood near"; temporal clause, see on 40. Scan as *nāuĭm ūt*, because of the hiatus after *nauim*.
188	**confabulatust** = *confabulatus est* < *confabulor*, "talk with."
189	**eho tu**: "hey you!" Charinus now addresses Acanthio with a menacing voice. **quin cauisti ne eam uideret**: "why didn't you make sure he did not see her?"; *cauisti* governs a negative jussive clause (substantive clause of purpose, AG 563). **uerbero**: literally, "one who deserves a flogging"; "rascal"; frequently used for slaves, like *scelestus* in the following line.
190	**apstrudebas** < *abstrudo*, "conceal." **conspiceret** < *conspicio*, "look at." There is prosodic hiatus after *ne*.
191	**negotiosi ... negotiis**: "busy with business"; etymological figure (i.e., the use of two words from the same root for emphasis).
192	**armamentis complicandis, componendis**: "(to) folding up and putting away the tackle"; dative of the gerundives to express purpose after *studuimus* (AG 505).
193	**dum**: "while"; + (historical) present indicative for continued action in past time (AG 556). **lembo** < *lembus*, "small boat; skiff." **pauxillulo**: diminutive of *paucus*, modifying *lembo*.
194	**quisquam**: "anyone." **conspicatust** < *conspicor*, "notice." **donec in nauim subit**: "until he boarded the ship."
195	**nequiquam**: "in vain." **supterfugi** < *supterfugio*, "escape." Charinus dramatically addresses the sea, whose storms he safely escaped as a merchant, only to fall prey now to his father's schemes. **a tuis**: Scan as *ā tŭĭs* because of iambic shortening resulting from the accent on *tempestatibus*.
196	**tuto** < *tutus*, "safe."
197	**uerum**: "but in fact." **med** = *me*.

198	**loquere**: See on 137; followed by an indirect question *quid sit actum*.
	porro: "then; next."
199-200	For the double line number see on 79-80.
	rogitare: See on 165.
	quoia= *cuius*; indirect question.
	ilico: "on the spot; instantly."
201	**occucurri** < *occurro*, "run up."
	interpello: "I interrupt."
	ancillam: "as a maid servant"; predicate to *illam* after *emisse*.
202	**emisse** (< *emo*): See on Argumentum I 2; infinitive in indirect statement, depending on *interpello*.
	uisun= *uisusne* (*est*).
203	**subigitare**: "to dishonor, to touch, to pet." This is an ironic comment from Acanthio, who calls Demipho *scelestus*, a word reserved for slaves.
204	**mirum quin me subigitaret**: "it is a miracle he did not touch me"; an indirect question introduced by *quin* (Bennett 1.329).
205	**quod guttatim contabescit, quasi in aquam indideris salem**: "which [i.e., my heart] withers away drop by drop, as if you put salt into water." *quasi* introduces a clause of conditional comparison (AG 524); *indideris* < *indo*, "put into, add."
206	**em**: See on 149.
209	**mendacium**: "lie."
213	Word order: *ne suspicio prehendat patrem ut res gesta sit*; *prehendat* < *prehendo*, "catch, take hold of." The *ne* clause is of fear, while *ut* introduces an indirect question.
214	<**quaeso**>: "please."
215	**suspicari** < *suspicor*, "suspect"; scan *num* with prosodic hiatus and *esse* with iambic shortening of the penultimate syllable.
216	**quin**: "in fact."
	quidque: "whatever."
	ut dicebam: "as I was saying"; for the correlative *ut* see on 45.
	uerum: sc. *est*, "the truth is."
216-217	**ut tibi quidem / uisus est**: "at least as he seemed to you."
	non: sc. *solum uisus est mihi*.

219	**istac**: sc. *uia*.
	commodum: "just at that time."
	obuiam uenies patri: "you will meet your father"; *obuiam* + dative, "in the path of."
220	**exanimatum**: "upset."
221	**unde emeris, quanti emeris**: indirect questions with perfect subjunctive depending on *rogitabit*. *quanti*: "for how much"; genitive of value.
222	**timidum**: in apposition with *te*.
	hac: sc. *uia*.
	potius: "rather."
223	**praecucurri** < *praecurro*, "run ahead, first."
	ea gratia: "for this reason."
224	**opprimeret** < *opprimo*, "catch unawares" (*OLD opprimo* 7).
	electaret (sc. *ueritatem*) < *electo*, "entice out (the truth); bring out (the truth)."

ACT II SCENE i
Demipho enters puzzled because of a dream, which he explains as it suits him best. This dream bears resemblance to Daemones' dream in Plautus' *Rudens* (593-614).
Meter: Iambic Senarii. See Introduction, Meter Cb 1.1.

¯ ¯ | ˘ ¯ | ¯   ¯ | ¯   ˘ ˘ | ¯   ˘ | ˘ ¯
miris modis di // ludos faciunt hominibus

225	**miris modis**: "in marvellous ways"; ablative of manner.
	di= *dei* < *deus*.
226	**somnia**: "dreams."
	danunt= *dant*. See Introduction, Language B 2h.
227	**uelut**: "just as."
228	**egi satis**: "I was hard pressed; I was anxious" (*OLD satis* 5).
	exercitus < *exerceo*, "vexed, harassed."
229	**mercari ... mihi**: "to have bought (for) myself."
	capram: "she-goat."
230	Word order: *ne* (sc. *illa capra*) *quam capram ante domi habui* (i.e., *uxor mea*) *ei* (sc. *caprae*) *noceret*. *capram* (the subject of *noceret*) has been attracted into the case of the relative pronoun *quam* (AG 306a note). The she-goat already in Demipho's house is his own wife.

231 **neu**= *ne-ue*.
ambae: "both."
232 **posterius quam**= *postquam*.
mercatus fueram= *mercatus eram*. Plautus often uses *fui* and *fueram* instead of *sum* or *eram* in the perfect and pluperfect passive (Bennett 1.49), as intensified expressions in the popular language (AG 495 note).
233 **in custodelam simiae concredere**: "to entrust her to the care of a monkey."
234 **adeo**: "in fact." It emphasizes *ea simia* (*OLD* 8).
post hau multo: "not long afterwards." *multo* is an ablative of degree of difference (see on 69); *hau multo* forms a litotes (the affirming of a thing by denying its opposite).
235 **male ... precatur** < *male precor*, "curse" + dative; iambic shortening of *male*.
facit conuicium: "abuses (me)."
236 **illius opera atque aduentu caprae**: "because of the arrival and the activities of that she-goat" (*hysteron proteron*, AG 640). Scan *illī(u)s* as bisyllabic.
237 **flagitium et damnum fecisse**: "to have incurred disgrace and loss."
238 **seruandam**. "to be kept, protected"; future passive participle as predicate to *quam*.
239 **suai**= *suae* (archaic genitive, see Introduction, Language B 1a).
dotem < *dos*, "dowry."
ambedisse < *ambedo*, "eat"; see AG 201 for the irregular verb *edo*.
oppido: "completely."
240 **ut**: introduces an indirect question after *mirum* sc. *esse* ("amazing how"), with a perfect subjunctive *ambederit* in the following line. There is iambic shortening on *illud* (see on 120); the infinitive *uideri* depends on an implied *dico*.
241 **simiai**= *simiae*.
242 **instare factum** (sc. *esse*): "the monkey insisted that it had been done." *instare* is an historical infinitive (see on 46).
243 **properem** < *propero*, "hurry, act quickly." The future-more-vivid condition is in indirect discourse, with the present subjunctive in the protasis (*properem*) and the future

infinitive in the apodosis (*ducturum* sc. *esse*). In direct discourse the condition would read: *ni properabis, ducam* (AG 589a3).

244 **ad me domum**= *ad meam domum*.
intro: "inside."
ad uxorem: *ăd ŭxōrem* by iambic shortening.

245 **bene uelle** < *bene uolo*, "love, have good intentions towards"; + dative.
illi: sc. *caprae*.

246 **ast**: "but, however."
quoi commendarem: "to whom I might entrust"; relative clause of purpose. The antecedent of *quoi* is the unexpressed object of *habere*.

247 **quo magi'**: "all the more, therefore."
cura: "with anguish, stress"; ablative of means introducing the indirect question *quid facerem*.
cruciabar < *crucio*, "torment."

248 **haedus**: "young he-goat; kid."
adgredirier= *adgredi* (< *adgredior*): "approach." See Introduction, Language B 2c.

249 **infit**: "begins to speak"; see AG 204b for the defective verb *infio*.
sese: subject of *praedicare* (see on 34).

250 **coepit**: See on 42.
inridere (< *inrideo*): "mock."

251 **lugere** (<*lugeo*): "to grieve"; historical infinitive.
aegre pati: "be sad, feel distress"; historical infinitive.

252 **hoc quam ad rem credam pertinere somnium**: "what I should believe this dream means"; scan as *quăm ăd rēm*.

253 **nequeo inuenire**: "I am unable to find out."
nisi: "but; except that."
capram illam: object of the infinitive *inuenisse*, but it also functions as subject in the indirect questions of the following line. Here, as often, the subject of the indirect question is attracted into the main clause as object of the verb (*prolepsis*, see AG 576).

254 **quae sit, quid uoluerit**: indirect questions; *uoluerit* < *uolo*, "signify, mean" (*OLD uolo* 17).

255 **mane**: "in the morning."

255   **cum luci semul** (= *simul*): "at daybreak"; *luci* is a locative (Enk 62).
256   **transegi** < *transigo*, "carry through."
      atque= *ecce*, "forthwith, lo and behold" (*OLD atque* 6 and Lindsay, *Syntax* VIII.2).
257   **ex Rhodo**: Plautus occasionally uses a preposition with the name of an island, although the preposition is omitted in classical Latin. Contrast line 11 and note.
      quast= *qua est*; *qua* is an ablative of means. After *heri*, there is prosodic hiatus, making its last syllable short.
258   **conlibitumst**: "it was agreeable."
      illuc: "to that place" (adverb).
      nescioqui: "for one reason or another" (adverbial).
      uisere (< *uiso*): "to go and look."
259   **inscendi** < *inscendo*, "climb up; go on board."
      lembum: See on 193.
260   **illi**: See on 97. Scan as *ĭll(i)*.
262   **quam ego postquam aspexi**: "and after I saw her"; a connecting relative (see on 6).
      sanei= *sani*. It is a stock feature in Greek and Roman comedy to portray the love of the elderly father as an example of insanity.
263   **eodem pacto**: "in the same manner."
264   **olim**: "once."
265   **exemplum**: "manner" (*OLD exemplum* 7).
267   **ceterum**: "as for the rest; moreover."
      quanti: See on 221.
268   **profecto**: "assuredly."
270   **eos esse**: Scan with prosodic hiatus *ĕŏs ēssĕ*.
      deicam= *dicam*. See Introduction, Language B 2j.
271   **conticiscam** < *conticisco*, "keep silent."
      eccum (= *ecce eum*): "look at that man!"
      foras: "to the outside of the house; outside; out of doors"; accusative of place to which (AG 215.3).

ACT II SCENE ii
Demipho's neighbor Lysimachus approaches, giving instructions to his slave. But he soons enters into conversation with Demipho. The exchange between the two old men is typical of comic scenes, where

Plautus *Mercator*

one is always more reasonable than the other. In this case, Demipho thinks he is young again, only to be scolded by Lysimachus, who thinks his neighbor is insane.
Meter: Iambic Senarii. See Introduction, Meter Cb 1.1.

⏑ ‾ | ‾ ⏑ ‾ | ‾ ‾ | ‾ ‾ | ‾ ⏑ ‾
profect(o) eg(o) illunc // hircum castrari uolo

272 **hircum**: "he-goat."
273 **ruri**: locative (AG 427).
uobeis= *uobis*.
exhibet negotium: "causes trouble."
274 **illuc**= *illud*.
275 **quasi hircum**: modifies *me*.
276 **illius ... simiae**: "of that monkey"; *illī(u)s* is bisyllabic.
hic: Demipho points to Lysimachus.
partis (= *partes*) **ferat**: "that he may play the role of."
277 **i** (< *eo*): second person present active imperative.
rastros: "mattocks"; for *istos* see on 165.
uilico < *uilicus*, "the overseer of the estate; steward."
278 **Pisto**: The steward's name, Pistus, means "faithful" in Greek.
facito: "make sure to"; followed by a substantive result clause introduced by *ut* (see AG 568).
coram: "in person."
280 **ne me exspectet**: negative purpose clause.
mihi: dative of agent in the passive periphrastic *iudicandas* sc. *esse*.
281 **tris litis**: "three cases (matters of dispute)"; accusative plural.
iudicandas: "to be adjudicated"; < *iudico*, "judge, decide a case."
282 **ei**= *i* (see on 277).
adicere < *adicio*, "add."
numquid amplius: "there is nothing more, is there?"
283 **eugae**: "good day; be well."
284 **quod miserrumus**: sc. *sum*, "(it happens) that I am as miserable as I can be!"
285 **di melius faxint**: "may the gods make it better for you!"; the optative *faxint* is frequently employed in prayers (Introduction, Language B 2g). There is prosodic hiatus between *di* and *hoc* (with iambic shortening on *hŏc*).

286 **tibi esse operam**: "you can spare some time." *tibi* is a possessive dative.
287 **quamquam**: "although."
ueis= *uis*. See Introduction, Language B 2j.
288 **operam dare** (< *operam do*): "to give my attention, apply my efforts."
289 **experto**: "experienced"; modifying *mi*, dative after *praedicas*. Scan as *mĭ ĕxpērtō* (iambic shortening on *ex-*).
290 **quid ... aetatis**: "of what age?" *aetatis* is a partitive genitive.
Accherunticus: "ready for Acheron"; spelled with a double *c* for metrical purposes. Acheron was one of the rivers of the Underworld. The adjective vividly applies to Demipho's old age.
291 **decrepitus**: "very old, worn out."
peruorse= *peruerse*, "erroneously."
292 **puer**: Scan as *pŭĕr* or with synizesis as one syllable.
septuennis: "seven years old." Boys of that age started school for the first time; Demipho thinks he is reborn, that he is a seven year old boy who has just started learning grammar and writing, as he makes clear in 303-304.
sanun= *sanusne*.
293 **qui puerum te esse dicas**. "since you call yourself a boy"; relative clause of characteristic expressing cause (AG 535e).
294 **quid tu diceres**: "what you meant by your words"; indirect question, depending on *in mentem uenit* ("it crossed my mind").
295 **quom extemplo**= "as soon as."
sapit (< *sapio*): "is sensible."
296 **aiunt**: "they/people say" (AG 206a).
repuerascere: "to become a boy again."
297 **immo**: See on 164.
bis tanto ualeo quam ualui prius: "I am twice as strong as I was before."
298 **immo si scias**: "if only you knew" (*OLD immo* h).
300 **malae rei**: sc. *oculeis uideo*, "for something bad, naughty."
301 **fideliter**: "confidentially."
302 **audacter**: "with assurance."
sedulo: "carefully."
303 **ludum ... litterarium**: "grade school."

304	**ternas** (sc. *litteras*): "three letters," which correspond to the letters of the verb *amo*, a word that Demipho has apparently just learned from scratch!
305	**cano** < *canus*, "white, grey." **nequissume** (superlative < the indeclinable adjective *nequam*): "most worthless, vilest"; vocative.
306	**seu istuc**: The dipthong is shortened in prosodic hiatus before *istuc*, whose first syllable is short. **rutilum** (sc. *caput*): "red." **atrum** < *ater*, "black."
307	**ludificas** < *ludifico*, "mock, deceive." **heic**= *hic* (adverb).
308	**decide** < *decido*, "cut off." **collum**: "neck." **stanti**: sc. *mihi*; dative of disadvantage.
309	**cultrum** < *culter*, "knife." **seca** < *seco*, "cut."
310	**aurem** < *auris*, "ear." **nassum** < *nasus*, "nose." **labrum**: "lip."
312	**auctor sum ut tu me amando— enices**: "I vouch that you may kill me off... by loving." The apodosis of the conditional sentence is unexpected (παρὰ προσδοκίαν) and has a ridiculous effect: just when the spectators suspect that Demipho would ask Lysimachus to finish him off, if he does not speak the truth, Demipho asks his neighbor to kill him *amando*, with love. Thereby Plautus underscores the insanity of the older man's love.
313	**pictum**: "painted"; i.e., in a painting.
314	**meo animo**: "in my opinion." **uetulus**: "old."
315	**tantidemst quasi**: "is of just the same value as if"; *tantidem* is a genitive of value. **signum**: "painting, artwork."
316	**castigare** (< *castigo*): "rebuke." **cogitas** (< *cogito*): "you consider ways and means of."
317	**egon te**: iambic shortening of *egon*. **suscenseas** < *suscenseo*, "be angry"; + dative of person.
318	**fecere**= *fecerunt*.

318 **spectatei**= *spectati*, "prominent, famous."
319-320 **peccare … ignoscere … / amare:** These infinitives are verbal nouns as subjects of *est* (AG 452); < *pecco*, "sin" and < *ignosco*, "forgive."
320 **optingit:** "falls as one's lot"; prosodic hiatus after *ui*.
deum= *deorum*.
321 **ne sis me obiurga:** "please, don't scold me"; *ne* + present imperative to express prohibition in archaic Latin (AG 450a).
hoc= *huc*.
322 **quin:** See on 216.
322-323 **deteriorem:** sc. *me esse*; < *deterior*, "worse" (defective adjective, AG 130a).
ne di siuerint: "God forbid!" *siuerint* < *sino*, "allow."
324 **uide sis modo etiam:** "once again, please, are you quite sure?"
perdi' me: "you are killing me."
325 **numquid uis:** "do you want anything (else)?" "is that all?"; a conventional parting formula in Plautus.
327 **bene ambulato:** "walk well!" i.e., "farewell!" Lysimachus leaves from the left for the harbor.
328 **quin … quoque etiam:** "but even also."
mihi: possessive dative.
329 **nunc adeo:** "now, I tell you what!"; introduces energetic command.
optume: iambic shortening on *o-* because of the accent on *sed*.
330 **opperiar** (< *opperior*): "I will wait for."
hoc … mihi uiso opust: "I need to see to this"; *opus est* (see on 106) is used here with the perfect passive participle *uiso* (AG 411a and n.2).
331 **huic:** dative with *persuadere*; i.e., Charinus.
potis siem= *possim*.
332 **ut illam uendat neue det matri suae:** "that he should sell her and that he should not give her to his mother"; *neue* is used here instead of *neque*.
333 **ei dono:** sc. *ei (matri) eam (ancillam) dono*; *ei* is a dative of reference and *dono* a dative of purpose.
aduexe= *aduexisse* (syncopated form).
praecauto opust: "there is need of caution" (see on 330).
334 Word order: *ne hic sentiat aliqua me illam animum adiecisse*.

illam me animum adiecisse: "that I have set my mind on her"; *adicio animum* is often constructed with the dative, but here with an accusative (*OLD adicio* 2b).
aliqua: "somehow."

ACT II SCENE iii
Charinus sings a *canticum* (335-363). He is very distressed since his father has already seen his girlfriend. The *canticum* is followed by a recitative, the exchange between father and son.
Meter: 335-336; 338; 340; 342-355; 357-358; 360-361: Bacchic Tetrameters (Intro Meter Cb 3.2)

⏑ − −│⏑ ⏑ ⏑−│− − −│ ⏑ − −
homo me miserior nullust aequ(e) opinor

337; 339: Anapestic Dimeters (Intro Meter Cb 3.3)

⏑ ⏑ −│⏑ ⏑ −│ ⏑ ⏑ −│− −
satin quidquid est quam r(em) ager(e) occepi

341; 356; 359; 362-363: Trochaic Octonarii (Intro Meter Cb 2.2 for scansion of 341)

364-468: Trochaic Septenarii (Intro Meter Cb 2.1)
⏑ ⏑ −│− −│− ⏑│− −│− ⏑│− −│− −
quid illuc est quod solus secum :: fabulatur filius

335   **me**: ablative of comparison.
336   **quoi**: dative with *aduorsa*.
      sempiterna: "everlasting."
337   **satin**= *nonne*; *satin* functions as an interrogative particle in colloquial Latin.
338   **proprium**: "certain, constant"; predicate to *quod cupio*. Scan with a long penultimate.
      euenire (< *euenio*): "happen, turn out."
      quod cupio: in apposition to *quam rem agere occepi*.
339   **obicitur** < *obicio*, "be thrown before someone, be presented to someone, occur"; + dative. For scansion see Introduction, Meter Cb 3.3.
340   **comprimit** < *comprimo*, "curb, subdue, hinder."

341 **animi causa**: "for myself"; *animus* here is a substitute for the speaker.
pretio: ablative of means or price. For scansion see Introduction, Meter Cb 2.2.
342 **ratus**: sc. *sum*, followed by indirect statement <*me*> *posse habere*.
clam patrem: See on 43.
343 **resciuit**: See on 107. Notice the emphasis on the parataxis (arrangement side by side) of the verbs connected with *et*.
344 **quid loquar**: "what I should say," "what to say"; indirect question introduced by *cogitatumst*. *quom roget* is a temporal *cum* clause with the subjunctive *roget* by attraction to *loquar*.
345 Charinus' confusion is described in terms of ten conflicting thoughts struggling in his mind at the same time. Notice the alliteration and word play with *incerti certant*.
346 **consili**: partitive genitive after *quid*.
347 **meost**: Pronounce as one syllable by synizesis.
error: "doubt, hesitation."
348 **perplacet**: "pleases exceedingly."
348-349 **dum ... / dum**: "sometimes ... sometimes."
349 **poti'**= *potis essè*, i.e., *posse*.
350 **induci** < *induco*, "mislead, seduce."
352 **quem ad modum**: "how; of what kind." Scan as *quĕm ăd mŏd(um)*. The subjunctive *existumet* is the apodosis of the mixed condition (protasis: *si dico* in 351).
353 **uenum**: "for sale."
asportet < *asporto*, "transport."
354-355 For the double line, see note on 79-80.
saeuo' quam sit, domo doctus: "how harsh he is, from my own experience"; *saeuo'*= *saevus* (sc. *pater*).
356 **hoccinne**= *hoc + ce + ne*, pleonastic strengthening of *hoc*. The infinitive *amare* is the subject of the verb *est* (see on 319-320).
357 **iam**: prosodic hiatus.
inuitum: "against my will."
domo extrusit ab se: pleonasm with two ablatives of separation (*domo, ab se*). See the Prologue, where Charinus recounts why his father sent him away to become a merchant;
extrusit: "expelled."

358   **mercatum**: supine of purpose.
         hoc malum: i.e., falling in love.
359   **ubi ... uincat**: This temporal clause has conditional force (future-less-vivid).
         aegritudo: See on 19.
         amoeni < *amoenus*, "pleasant"; partitive genitive.
360   **nequiquam**: "in vain."
         abdidi < *abdo*, "hide."
         apscondidi < *abscondo*, "conceal."
         apstrusam habebam: "I had her hidden"; *habeo* with a perfect passive participle is equivalent to the perfect active tense, i.e., "I hid her" but shows the continued effect of the action of the verb (AG 497b).
361   **musca**: "fly."
362   **quin**: A result clause after a negative is often introduced by *quin* (AG 559.1).
363   **qui rebus meis confidam**: "how I may put trust in my situation." This is an indirect question after *spes certast*; *confidam* + dative.
364   **quid illuc est quod**: See on 120.
         fabulatur < *fabulor*, "speak, talk."
365   **nescioqua re**: "for one reason or another"; scan as *nēscĭōquā*.
         attatae: exclamation of despair.
366   **hicquidem**: Scan as *hĭcquĭd(em)*.
367   **gnate mi**: vocative; < *gnatus*, "son."
         recte: "that's all right"; it is used to avoid giving a straight answer (*OLD recte* 10b).
368   **sed istuc**: Scan as *sĕd ĭstūc* (iambic shortening).
         commutatust < *commuto*, "change."
369   **nescioquid**: "something."
370   **poste**= *praeterea*, "besides."
         quieui < *quiesco*, "rest."
         mea ex sententia: "in my opinion; I think."
373   **palles** < *palleo*, "be pale."
         sapias < *sapio*, "be wise."
         decumbas: See on 99.
374   **praeuorti** < *praeuertor*, "give precedence to"; + dative.
375   **perendie**: "the day after tomorrow."
376   **omnis sapientis**: accusative plural, alternative ending in *–is*.

377 **age igitur**: "well, then."
aduorsari ... aduorsum: pleonastic use of the preposition *aduersum* after the verb *aduersor*.
378 In his aside to the spectators, Charinus claims he is safe, for the moment; *isti* is here a demonstrative of the second person that does not involve contempt.
379 **seuocat** < *seuoco*, "separate." Demipho also murmurs this to himself, wondering about Charinus' strange behavior. Notice the pleonasm: *ille solus seuocat se a me*. Each protagonist hopes that the other knows nothing about the girl.
381 **quippe**: "certainly."
inepte: "inappropriately."
amantes ut solent: sc. *facere*.
382 **in tutost**: sc. *loco*.
sat= *satis*.
383 **quod**: "because"; the conditional sentence is present contrary-to-fact.
384 **amolior**: "remove."
385 **amicus**: "as a friend"; predicate nominative.
immo: "no, rather."
386 **paucula**: diminutive of *paucus*.
sciscitare < *sciscitio*, "ask."
387 **usquine**= *usque* + *ne*, "without an interruption."
388 **ut sum aduectus**: temporal *ut*.
nescioqui: See on 258.
389 **nausea**: ablative of cause.
factum: sc. *esse*.
apscesserit: See on 140.
390 **quid ais**: "what do you say (about the following)?"
ecquam < *ecquis*, "any?"
aduexti= *aduexisti*.
e Rhodo: For the use of the preposition see on 257.
391 **ut**: "how"; it introduces a direct question.
392 **morata** < *moratus*, "well-mannered."
melius: sc. *moratam esse*.
393 **uisast**: sc. *morata esse*.
eho= exclamation of surprise.
394 **ex usu nostro**: "advantageous; serviceable; useful for us."

395	**dignam**: "worthy (of)"; + ablative of specification (AG 418b), here *nostra ... domo*.
396	**ancilla**: ablative after *opust*.

396-398 **quae texat, quae molat.../...habeat**: relative clauses of characteristic expressing purpose (see on 75). In these lines, we get an idea of the usual daily work for slave girls.
texat < *texo*, "weave."
molat < *molo*, "grind."

397	**lignum**: "wood; timber."

caedat < *caedo*, "cut."
pensum: "stint," i.e., the amount of wool weighed out daily to be spun or woven.
aedis= *aedes* (in the plural), "house."
uorrat < *uorro*, "sweep."
uapulet: See on 167. Male and female slaves alike were subject to flogging.

398	**quae habeat**: prosodic hiatus after *quae*, whose syllable is shortened.

coctum < *coquo*, "cook"; for *habeo* with a participle see on 360.

399	**horunc**= *horum* + *ce*; partitive genitive.

nihilum= *nihil*.
admodum: "quite right."

401-402 **duas**: perfect subjunctive of *do*, instead of *dederis*; prohibition with *ne*.

403	**labefacto**: "shake, totter"; it is used transitively here. Demipho celebrates his victory with a side comment.

praeterii < *praetereo*, "omit."

404	Roman *matronae* used to have a slave follower (*comes*) when going out in public; *comes* is a predicate to *illa*. (Cf. Philemon fr. 115 K-A).
405	**sinam** < *sino*, "permit."

forma: See 13; scan *illa* with iambic shortening on *ill-*.
familias= *familiae*.

406	**flagitium**: "disgrace."

sei= *si*. This is a future-less-vivid conditional.
quando: "whenever"; + present subjunctive introduces a temporal indefinite clause (AG 514).
incedat < *incedo*, "walk."

407	**contemplent** < *contemplo*, "look at"; the subjunctive continues the future-less-vivid conditional implied by the *quando* clause. **conspiciant** < *conspicio*, "gaze upon." **nutent** < *nuto*, "nod." **nictent** < *nicto*, "wink." **sibilent** < *sibilo*, "whistle."
408	**uellicent** < *uellico*, "pinch." **molesti**: "harassing." **occentent** < *occento*, "serenade, sing (outside the door)"; + accusative.
409	**impleantur** <*impleo*, "fill"; + ablative of means (see AG 409a). **elegeorum**: "of love poems." **fores**: "doors." **carbonibus**: "pieces of charcoal (used for writing)," "writing." Lovers would write on the walls and doors the names of their beloved and other ditties.
410	**maledicentes**: "slanderous."
411	**obiectent** < *obiecto*, "accuse, charge"; + dative of the person charged. **lenocinium**: "pandering." **eost**: i.e., the people's accusations.
412	**qui**: "somehow." **recte**: See on 367. There is hiatus after *tĭbĭ*, and in the sixth foot there is a *breuis in longo*, resulting in an iamb *(-bĭ ād-)* by exception.
413	**quid illa**: Scan with iambic shortening of *ill-*.
414	**uiraginem** < *uirago*, "a man-like woman."
415	**ut ... addecet**: "as it befits"; + accusative. **Syram aut Aegyptiam**: Following the stereotype, Demipho categorizes female slaves from the East as mannish and ugly. Lysimachus' wife has a slave named Syra. See Act IV.
416	**molet ... coquet ... pensum**: See on 396-398. **conficiet** < *conficio*, "complete." **pinsetur** < *pinso*, "strike." **flagro** < *flagrum*, "flogging."
417	**propter**: "on account of"; + accusative.
418	**reddatur** < *reddo*, "return."

minime gentium: "not for the world!"

419 **dixit se redhibere**: sc. *eam*, "he said that he would take her back"; *redhibere* (literally, "take back a defective product") is a technical term for returning slaves to their seller.

420 **litigari** < *litigo*, "go to court."
autem: "moreover."
accusari fidem: "your trustworthiness to be blamed."

421 **multo ... mauolo**: "I much prefer"; *multo* is an ablative of degree of difference.
facere damni: "to incur some loss"; *damni* is a partitive genitive.

422 **opprobramentum**: "scandal."
ecferri < *ecfero*: "to be publicized." Demipho seems to imply that the seller would not take the girl back anyway; therefore, they would have to resolve the matter through litigation, thereby exposing the scandal of bringing a prostitute into Demipho's (otherwise) honorable house. This would damage Charinus' *fides* for ever.

423 **tibi**: dative of advantage (AG 376).
luculente= *cum lucro*, "with profit."

424-25 **dum ... ne**: "provided that not" (proviso clause).
minoris (sc. *pretii*): "for a lesser price" (genitive of value). There is prosodic hiatus between *quam* and *ego*.

426 **illam**: direct object of *emerem*.

427 **ad istanc faciem**: "(a girl) of that appearance." There is a hiatus after *emerem*, because of the pause and another hiatus after *faciem*, at the *diaeresis* of both 427 and 428.

429 **uiginti minis**: The sum of twenty to thirty *m(i)nae* seems to be a common price for purchasing slaves, as we can gather from Plautus' plays.

431 **inquam**: "I say"; for this defective verb, see AG 206b.
quid dicturus sum: indirect question with the indicative.

432 **accudere**: "to mint up, to add." Both Demipho and Charinus bid for the girl on behalf of their imaginary friends.

433 **uortisti**= *uertisti*. Demipho pretends to be part of an imaginary auction, staring at an imaginary buyer who is now offering more.
qui emit: prosodic hiatus after *qui*, whose syllable is shortened before *ĕmĭt*.

433   **ubinamst is homo gentium**: "where in the world is this man?"
434   **eccillum**= *ecce illum*.
        iubet: Scan as *iŭbĕt*.
436   **di infelicent**: "may the gods make him unhappy"; optative subjunctive (AG 441).
        ibidem: "in that very moment."
437   **adnutat** < *adnuto*, "nod."
        addam: i.e., *ut addam*.
438   **commodis poscit**: "he asks with a good offer."
439   **illic**= *ille + ce*.
        pollicitust < *polliceor*, "bid."
440   **nihili facio**: "I count it for nothing; I don't care"; for *nihili* see on 125.
        non centum datur: "she is not given (to him) for a hundred."
441   **potine ut ne licitere**: "are you able not to bid"; negative substantive clause of purpose. *ut ne* is common in negative purpose clauses in Plautus; *licitere* < *licitor*, "bid" (frequentative form of *liceor*); second person singular present subjunctive.
442   **quoi**: "on whòse behalf"; short syllable in prosodic hiatus, also in 444 and 447.
443   **quod posces feres**: "you will get what you ask"; i.e., name a price and you will get it. Scan *īllī(u)s* as bisyllabic.
444   **ecflictim**: "to destruction."
447   **quoi ... do hanc operam**: "for whom I provide this service," i.e., for whom I buy this girl.
448   **quiesce**: Scan as one syllable; the final *-e* is elided; *-ie-* are treated as one syllable by synizesis.
        rem ego: prosodic hiatus.
        quid ais: See on 390.
449   **non ego illam mancupio accepi**: "I did not purchase her with legal rights." Charinus could not sell a slave who is still legally under someone else's ownership. *Man(i)cupium* refers to the transfer of legal ownership, of a slave in this case, and to the guarantee that the person sold is truly of slave status.

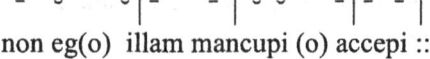

non eg(o) illam mancupi (o) accepi ::

Plautus *Mercator*

˘ ˘ ‾ | ‾ ˘ ˘|‾ ˘|‾
sed ill(e) ill(am) accipiet sine

[Note the iambic shortening of some of the demonstrative pronouns.]

sine: "let go."

451 **post autem**: "after all."
mihi: dative of possession.
cum alio: prosodic hiatus after *cum*.

452 **quid sit ei animi**: "what he thinks; how he feels."
uenirene eam uelit an non uelit: double indirect question; *uenire* < *ueneo*.

453 **qui non uelit**: "who may not wish."

454 **quid id mea refert**: "why does it concern me?"; for the ablative *mea* with *refert* see AG 355a.
in manu: "in his power; his property." Since a slave belongs to the master, s/he is in the master's possession.

456 **tu emis**: prosodic hiatus, making *tu* short.

457 **necne**: "or not."
abalienarier < *abalieno*, "transfer (property) to another legally; give up possession of"; present passive infinitive.

458 **si emetur, tum uolet**: sc. *illam abalienarier*; future-more-vivid condition. Demipho's logical question cannot possibly be answered by Charinus: how could the person who shares the girl with Charinus not object to her being sold to Charinus' "imaginary" bidder but on the other hand object to Demipho's buyer?

459 **nihil agis**: "you are wasting your time"; prosodic hiatus at the *diaeresis*.

461 **certumnest**: "is it final?"
censen= *nonne censes*?

462 **uenibit**: future of *ueneo*.
illo: "to that place."

463 Demipho refers to Charinus' comment in 374, when he said he was about to take care of business.

464 **at me incusato: te fecisse sedulo** (sc. *dicito*): "of course, blame me (and say that) you have made a sincere effort." For the use of *incusato* see Enk 98; prosodic hiatus after *me*.

465 **bitas** < *baeto* or *bito*, "go"; prohibition with *ne*.
auscultabitur: "it will be heeded."

466-68 Demipho talks to himself as he sets out for the harbor, while Charinus is left behind on stage in despair.

466 **cauto opust**: "I must make sure, I must take care"; for the participle with *opust* see 330.

468 **dudum**: "a while ago."
occidi < *occido*, "die, perish."

ACT II SCENE iv
After Charinus' dramatic monologue, Eutychus, Lysimachus' son, comes in. He will play a significant role in the resolution of the play. Meter: Trochaic Septenarii. See Introduction, Meter Cb 2.1.

```
 -  ˘| -    -| ˘  ˘ |  - -    |  -    - | -   - | -  ˘| -
```
Pentheum diripuiss(e) aiunt :: Bacchas nugas maxumas

469 Pentheus opposed Bacchus' cult in Thebes and was torn into pieces by his own mother and aunts. Charinus compares his situation to Pentheus' (cf. Euripides' *Bacchae*).
diripuisse < *diripio*, "tear into pieces."
Bacchas: subject of the infinitive *diripuisse* in indirect statement after *aiunt*.
nugas: "nonsense."

470 **praeut quo pacto ego diuorsus distrahor**: "in comparison to the way in which I am pulled asunder in pieces." Scan *fuisse* with synizesis on –*ui*-.

471 **qur**= *cur*.
ueivo= *uiuo*.
quid mihist in: Scan as *quīd mĭhĭst īn* (iambic shortening of the ultima in *mihist*).
boni: partitive genitive.

472 **toxico** < *toxicum*, "poison"; ablative of means.

473 **quando id mi adimitur qua caussa uitam cupio uiuere**: "since this is taken away from me, for the sake of which I desire to live my life"; *mi* is a dative of separation.
uitam ... uiuere: etymological figure (see on 191).

475 **tuos**= *tuus*.
simul: "also."

477 **auscultaui**: "I heard (with attention)."

479 **tuam amicam**: For scansion see note on 181.
tuis ingratieis: "to your discomfort"; ablative of manner.

Plautus *Mercator*

480 **plurumum**: "the most," i.e., everything.
481 **tute**: emphatic *tu*.
ipsus= *ipse*.
narrasti= *narrauisti* (syncopated form).
satine ut: "in fact how; can it be that."
oblitus fui= *oblitus sum* (see note on 232); < *obliuiscor*, "forget."
482 **consulo**: "consult, seek advice from."
483 **me**: instead of *ego*, which we would expect in the indirect question (*prolepsis*; see on 253).
potissumum: "in preference to all else."
484 **caue tu istuc deixis**: "don't say that!" *deixis*= *dixeris*, perfect active subjunctive. For *caue* in prohibitions see on 113.
ueis= *uis*.
485 **uin**= *uisne*.
patri sublinere ... os tuo < *sublino os* + dative: "smear someone's face, make a fool of someone." The phrase acquired its figurative meaning from the practical joke of smearing someone's face while he was sleeping (*OLD sublino*).
pulchre: "perfectly, very well."
sane: "if you will; then; so; surely."
486 **eam** < *eo*, "go."
qui (sc. *uolo eas*) **potius quam uoles**: "how do I wish you to go rather than fly?"; *uoles* < *uolo*, "fly." The phrase is equivalent to a command (for *potius quam* subjunctive clauses, see Bennett 1.322).
eximam < *eximo*, "set free, save."
487 **qui** (sc. *uolo eam eximas*) **potius quam auro expendas**: "how do I wish you to free her rather than weigh her out for gold?" (i.e., pay her weight in gold); *expendas* < *expendo*, "measure by weight, pay, ransom."
unde erit: "where will it be from?" i.e., "where will I get it from?"
488 In *Iliad* 24, Priam ransoms the body of his son Hector from Achilles by paying in gold (24.232) the amount of ten talents (cf. 703 for the same amount of money).
Acchillem: In Plautus, Achilles is spelled with a double *c* for metrical purposes.

Plautus *Mercator*

488	**mihi det**: jussive clause after *orabo*.
	expensus fuit= *expensus est*. The line is thought to echo a similar one from Diphilus' Ἔμπορος fr. 32 K-A. The case of Priam and Achilles belongs to a stock of exemplary stories of ransom.
489	**expetam** < *expeto*, "ask, look for."
490	**tanti, quanti**: genitives of value.
490-91	**auctarium / adicito**: "raise his bid."
491	**uel mille nummum**: "even a thousand coins."
492	**quid ais**: See on 390.
493	**exquiretur** < *exquiro*, "search out" (*hysteron proteron*).
494	**muto imperas**: "you order a mute person."
495	**ut aliud cures**: substantive clause of purpose after *potin*.
496	**non ... possum**: sc. *bene ualere*. Charinus is picking up Eurychus' words.
	priu'quam ... redieris: *priusquam* with a future perfect here.
497	**melius sanus sis**: "better, you should be reasonable," i.e., it would be better, if you should remain calm and reasonable.
498	**maneto me**: "wait for me."
	face cum praeda recipias (sc. *te*): "make sure you come back with the booty"; *face= fac*, with a substantive clause of result, here without *ut*. In Plautus, we often find the colloquial Latin usage of active verbs without the reflexive pronoun (*recipias* sc. *te*), a substitute for the Greek Middle Voice (Lindsay, *Syntax* V.4).

ACT III SCENE i
Lysimachus, Demipho's neighbor, comes back from the harbor with Pasicompsa. In Greek, the name Pasicompsa means "elegant among all." The plot thickens, as Lysimachus mistakenly thinks Pasicompsa has already been having an affair with Demipho for two years. Meter: Iambic Septenarii. See Introduction, Meter Cb 1.2.

⏑ ‾| ⏑ ‾| ⏑ ⏑ ‾ |⏑‾ |‾ ‾|‾ ‾ ‾ |⏑ ‾|‾
amic(e) amic(o) operam dedi :: uicinus quod rogauit

499	**amice**: adverb. Notice the alliteration *amice amico*.
	quod: The antecedent is *hoc mercimonium*, "this merchandise."

- 500 **mea es**: Lysimachus addresses his newly acquired "property," Pasicompsa. See note on 449 for *man(i)cupium*.
  sequere: present imperative.
- 501 **ne plora**: "don't cry!"
  facis: The last syllable is long because of its position before the *diaeresis*. See Introduction, Meter Cb 1.2.
  corrumpis < *corrumpo*, "spoil."
  talis: accusative plural, modifies *oculos*.
- 502 **quin**: "in fact."
  tibi quod rideas magis est, quam ut lamentere: "it is preferable for you to laugh rather than to cry." The conjunction *quod* + subjunctive, instead of *ut*, is unusual (Lindsay, *Syntax* VIII.2); *lamentere*: second person present subjunctive.
- 503 **amabo**: "please"; the word is used only by women or men who address women.
  ecastor: This is a frequent interjection for women in comedy (see note on 6).
  exquire quiduis: "ask whatever you wish."
- 504 **tene ego**: sc. *emerim*.
  imperetur: subjunctive by attraction to *facias* (see note on 36).
- 505 **item quod tu mihi si imperes, ego faciam**: "which I would do likewise, should you order me." Lysimachus is falling for Pasicompsa's fine looks and would like more than just her services as a slave.
- 506 **pro copia**: "as my circumstances allow" (*OLD copia* 5c). Pasicompsa exploits Lysimachus' sexual insinuations in her own reply, as she suspects that she could take advantage of the old man's lust for her.
- 507 **laboriossi nil ... quicquam operis**: "not very hard work."
- 508 **namque edepol**: sc. *recte facis*.
  baiiolare (< *baiiolo*): "carry weight."
- 509 **pecua** < *pecus* or *pecu*, "flock."
  pascere < *pasco*, "feed, rear." The last syllable is long before the *diaeresis*.
  nutricare < *nutrico*, "nurse." Pasicompsa presents a picture of her abilities that sharply contrasts with the ideal servant

	portrayed by Demipho in 416. She cannot perform any of the traditional duties of an *ancilla*.
511	**qui**: See on 183.
illim: "from that place, thence."
malis: sc. *puellis*. Pasicompsa says that usually women of bad reputation fared well in Rhodes, a place well-known for its prostitutes.
511a	This line was added to soften the transition from 511 to 512. Lysimachus tries to calm Pasicompsa by promising her a better life, but Pasicompsa complains that daily occupation with housework does not necessarily constitute a better lifestyle.
hic: "here"; *bonis*: sc. *puellis*.
nulli: modifies *mulieri*.
513	**mos meust ut**: "it is my habit to"; + substantive result clause (AG 571).
quod ego omnis scire credam: "[something] which I believe everyone knows"; the *quod* relative clause is object of *praedicem*.
514	**oratio pluris est huius quam quanti haec emptast**: "her way of speaking is worth more than the price for which she was bought." *huius* is possessive genitive with *oratio*; *pluris, quanti* are genitives of value.
515	**roganti**: sc. *tibi*; indirect object to *respondebo*.
516	**tibi**: dative of possession.
Pasicompsae: dative in apposition with *tibi* (AG 373a).
517	**inditumst** < *indo*, "give."
518	**possin tu, sei ussus uenerit**: "would you be able, should the need arise"; an uncommon type of future-less-vivid condition, with a perfect subjunctive in the protasis and a present subjunctive in the apodosis (AG 514 B2b).
subtemen: "yarn."
tenue < *tenuis*, "fine (of texture)"; predicate accusative to *subtemen*.
nere (< *neo*): "spin." Notice the multiple alliterations: *ussus subtemen tenue nere*.
519	**uberius**: "more fruitfully; in greater abundance."
Lysimachus' words are loaded with sexual connotations: the

act of spinning (*tenue, uberius nere*) becomes equivalent to intercourse.

520 **de lanificio**: "concerning weaving."
una aetate: "of the same age"; ablative of specification (AG 418). Pasicompsa does not fail to realize the obscenity of Lysimachus' words and responds in the same fashion.

521 **bonae te frugi arbitror**: "I think you are a virtuous girl"; *bonae frugi* ("virtuous, thrifty" *OLD frux* 5b) is a dative of purpose (and later becomes an indeclinable adjective, AG 122b).
iam inde: "moreover."

522 **docta didici**: "I have learned well and haven't forgotten." There is a sexual double-entendre in *facere officium* ("do one's duty"); see J. N. Adams, *The Latin Sexual Vocabulary* (London 1982), 163-64.

523 **operam accusari non sinam meam**: "I will not allow anyone to complain about my work." Scan *mĕ(am) ĕm ĭs-* as tribrach.

524 **ouem** < *ouis*, "sheep."
eccillam= *ecce illam*. Lysimachus points to Demipho's house.
natam: modifies *ouem*, "born."
annos sexaginta: "for sixty years; sixty years old"; accusative of time (AG 423-424).

525 **peculiarem** < *peculiaris*, "to be your own (private property)."
uetulam: See on 314.
generis graeci: Greek sheep are supposed to produce the best wool. There is a derogatory sense, however, in this description, as for the Roman audience, the Greek origin of the sheep would also refer to the low moral standards that Demipho displays.

526 **perbona**: "extremely good."
tondetur < *tondeo*, "shear"; the present indicative is used with a future force.
scite: "cleverly, neatly" (adverb from *scio*).

527 **gratum habebo**: "I will be grateful for"; + accusative (*quidquid est*).

528 Lysimachus is flattered that Pasicompsa is going to render her services to him, instead of Demipho.

528 **frustra sis** < *frustra sum*, "be mistaken"; *ne frustra sis*, *ne arbitrere* (= *arbitreris*) are prohibitions with *ne* + present subjunctive.
529 **quoia**: "whose?"
redempta's rursum: "you have been bought again."
530 **ego te**: iambic shortening of *ego* before *te*.
531 **sei mecum seruatur fides**: "if his promise to me is kept." Pasicompsa thinks that Charinus is the *erus* to whom Lysimachus refers in 529. Pasicompsa and Lysimachus will be at cross purposes for the rest of the scene.
bono animo es: "cheer up"; *es* is second person present imperative of *sum*.
532 **deperit** < *depereo*, "be desperately in love."
atque= *et tamen*.
533 **biennium**: "two years."
rem= *amorem*.
coëpit: Scan as trisyllabic, *cŏēpĭt*.
534 Scan *īllī(u)s* as bisyllabic.
535 **rem habet**: prosodic hiatus of *rem*.
536 **coniurauimus** < *coniuro*, "take an oath together."
536-36a ˘ ˘ ‾ | ‾ ‾ | ‾ ‾ | ˘ ‾ | ˘ ˘ ‾ | ˘ ‾ | ˘ ‾ | ‾
et inter nos coniurauimus :: ego c(um) ill(o) et ille mecum

˘ ˘ ‾ | ˘ ‾ ‾ | ‾ ˘ ‾ ‾ ‾ |
ego cum uir(o) et ill' cum muliere ::

˘ ˘ ‾ | ‾ ‾ ‾ | ‾ | ‾
nisi c(um) ill(o) aut ille mecum

537 **neuter ... caput limaret**: "that neither would embrace [someone else]"; a substantive stipulative clause after *coniurauimus* (Bennett 1.267). *limare caput* (sc. *cum aliquo*): "to rub heads with," i.e., "to embrace, kiss."
stupri < *stuprum*, "illicit sexual intercourse (of any sort)"; *stuprum* applies to women who are not married at the time of the act.
538 **cubet** < *cubo*, "sleep"; potential subjunctive.
amabo: "excuse me?"

539 **nolim quidem**: "I wish he were not!" There is hiatus after *quidem*, which has a long ultima because of its position at the *diaeresis*.
peiierauit < *peiiero* or *periuro*, "commit perjury; lie under oath."
540 Lysimachus is making fun of Pasicompsa, calling Demipho a *puer* (see also on 292).
541 **illi**: dative of disadvantage.
hau ... diust: litotes.
exciderunt < *excido*, "fall out"; the double entendre here is that Demipho is so young that he has just changed teeth, whereas in reality he has lost all his teeth because of age. See Introduction, Meter Cb 1.2 for scansion.
542 **hunc ... diem unum**: accusative of extent of time (AG 423-424).
543 **apud me**: "at my house."
praehiberem < *praehibeo*, "provide."
uxor: sc. *mea*.

ACT III SCENE ii
Demipho returns from the harbor as Lysimachus and Pasicompsa enter the former's house.
Meter: Iambic Senarii. See Introduction, Meter Cb 1.1.

```
 ‒     ‒  ˘ ‒   ˘ ˘ ‒  ‒   ‒  ‒  ‒   ˘ ‒
tand(em) impetrau(i) ut // egomet me corrumperem
```

544 **impetraui** < *impetro*, "manage, achieve."
me corrumperem: Demipho rejoices, as he is finally going to have an opportunity to cheat on his wife.
546 **antiqua**: "my old behavior." Demipho refers to his early days as a bachelor, before he got married.
recolam < *recolo*, "resume, practise again."
seruibo < *seruio*, "gratify"; + dative. For the future ending see Introduction, Language B 2k.
547 **breue**: predicate to *spatium*.
548 **delectauero** < *delecto*, "amuse"; scan *uŏlŭptātĕ* with iambic shortening of the antepenultimate because of the accent on the penultimate.

549 **nam hanc se bene habere aetatem nimiost aequius**: "for it is more than fair at this age to have fun."
550 **integer**: "fresh, new."
551 **rei ... quaerundae**: "to make money"; dative (with *operam dare*) of the gerundive to express purpose.
     conuenit: "it is appropriate"; + infinitive.
552 **demum**: "finally."
553 **conloces** < *conloco*, "settle"; *conloces, ames* are jussive subjunctives.
     dum potest: "while it is possible."
     lucrum: "profit."
554 **quod uiuis**: "the fact that you are alive"; subject of *est* in the previous line; a *quod* substantive clause (AG 572).
     facteis= *factis*.
     persequar < *persequor*, "follow up."
555 **ad med ... domum**= *ad me*, "to my house."
     inuisam < *inuiso*, "go to see."
556 **iam dudum**: For *iam dudum* with the present tense see on 138.
     essuriens < *e(s)surio*, "be hungry."
557 **iurgio**: "quarrel"; ablative.
558 **postremo**: "finally."
     utut: emphatic *ut*.
559 **conueniam** < *conuenio*, "meet."
560 **aliquas**: modifies *aedis*.
     conducat < *conduco*, "rent."
561 **ubi habitet**: "where she can stay"; relative clause of purpose (AG 531.2).

ACT III SCENE iii
Lysimachus comes out of his house, leaving Pasicompsa with some last piece of advice. Demipho plans a dinner party, a common element in Roman comedy. Meter: Iambic Senarii. See Introduction, Meter Cb 1.1.

```
   ⁻  ⁻|        ˘   ⁻|⁻         ⁻|⁻ ⁻|⁻   ⁻|˘ ⁻
adduc(am) eg(o) illum // i(am) ad te si conuenero
```

565 **quod opust facto facito ut cogites**: "make sure to think what needs to be done."

567	**illo**: "to that place."
	itane uero: "is that really so?"
	ueruex: "castrated ram." Lysimachus reproaches Demipho for his impotence in love at this old age.
	intro eas: Lysimachus' insinuates intercourse by using this formula, in a disparaging tone; *eas* < *eo*, "go." Scan with iambic shortening of *ĭll(o)*.
568	**quid aliud faciam**: direct question with deliberative subjunctive (AG 444).
	ades: sc. *animo* "pay attention."
569	**prius etiamst**: "there is also a thing first."
570	**ieris** (< *eo*): future perfect.
	amplecti (< *amplector*): "embrace."
571	**ausculari**: archaic form of *osculari*, "kiss."
572	**meum animum gestas**: "you read my mind."
	quid acturus siem: "what I am going to do"; indirect question with the verb in the present subjunctive of the active periphrastic conjugation (*acturus sim*, AG 195).
573	**peruorse facies**: "you will do the wrong thing."
	quodne amem: sc. *id non osculer*, "what I love [I should not kiss]?"
	tanto minus: sc. *osculeris, si amas*, "you should kiss her much less, if you love her."
574	**iaiunitatis** < *iaiunitas*, "fasting, dryness." Notice the oxymoron with *plenus*.
	anima foetida: "of foul breath"; ablative of quality.
575	**hircosus**: "goaty."
	osculere= *osculeris*.
576	**excutias** < *excutio*, "shake out, force."
	mulieri: dative of separation.
577	**praemostras** < *praemo(n)stro*, "announce."
578	**censes** < *censeo*, "agree."
	coquom < *coquus* or *cocus*, "cook."
579	**arripiamus** < *arripio*, "catch."
	prandium: "meal."
	qui percoquat: "who could cook, to cook"; relative clause of purpose.
580	**apud te**: "at your house."

Plautus *Mercator*

580 **usque ad uesperum**: "until the evening." Scan: ĕm ĭstūc (iambic shortening).
581 **amatorie**: "like a lover"; scan ămătōrĭē.
582 **opsonium**: "grocery shopping."
583 **pulchre ut simus**: "so that we have a good time." The use of adverbs with *esse* is a feature of colloquial Latin (Lindsay, *Syntax* VI.1).
584 **illi**= *Pasicompsae*.
585 **praeter**: "except for"; + accusative.
587 **hic**: See on 116.
      offendat < *offendo*, "come upon."
      Demipho and Lysimachus exit to the right to go to the forum and take care of their business and shopping.

ACT III SCENE iv
This meeting between Eutychus and Charinus sets the rest of the play into motion, since Eutychus will put an end to Demipho's crazy infatuation with Pasicompsa at the end of the comedy.
Meter: Trochaic Septenarii. See Introduction, Meter Cb 2.1.

‾ ˘ ‾|˙ ˘|‾ ‾|‾ ‾ |˘ ˘ ‾|‾ ‾|‾
sumn(e) eg(o) homo miser, qui nusquam :: bene queo quiescere

588 **qui nusquam ... queo quiescere**: "since I am never able to rest"; a relative clause of characteristic expressing cause (iambic shortening of the ultima of *bene*).
589 **foris**: "outside"; locative.
590 **in pectore atque in corde**: This repeats the Homeric formula κατὰ φρένα καὶ κατὰ θυμόν.
      incendium: "flame, fire."
591 **defendant** < *defendo*, "ward off" (sc. *incendium*).
      ardeat < *ardeo*, "burn." Charinus believes that tears offer a relief to his pain and desperation.
592 **salutem**: "well-being."
      amisi < *amitto*, "let go, lose."
      redeat an non: "whether it (i.e., *salus*) will return or not."
593 **opprimit** < *opprimo*, "press on, hold fast."
      exsolatum= *exsulatum*, "to go into exile"; supine of purpose.
594 **sein**= *sin*, "if again."
595 **tamendem si**: "even if"; introduces a conditional with a

concessive force.
podagrosis pedibus: ablative of quality. The *podagra*, or gout, is a disease of the feet that makes the joints and toes bleed.

596 **potuit**: For the perfect indicative with *possum* in the apodosis of a contrary-to-fact condition see AG 517c; iambic shortening of the preposition *a* because of the accent on *iam* ("already").
illi: dative of possession.

597 **aduorsum**= *aduersum*, "in comparison to"; + accusative.

598 **ibo obuiam** < *eo obuiam*, "go to meet."

599 **quod restat**: "the fact that he stops"; for the *quod* clause see on 554. Charinus breaks off in mid-sentence (*aposiopesis*).
ei: "alas."
disperii < *dispereo*, "be finished off."
ne utiquam: "not at all."

600 **tristis incedit**: Scan *trĭstĭs ĭncēdĭt* (iambic shortening of *in-*).
haereo: "I am unable to move" (*OLD haereo* 8).
quassat < *quasso*, "shake" (frequentative of *quatio*).

601 **recipias anhelitum**: "you catch your breath."

602 **hicine an apud mortuos**: "here or among the dead?"

603 **inmortalitas**: Charinus rejoices, since he thinks there is some hope left.

604 **pulchre os subleuit patri**: See on 485. For scansion see Introduction, Meter Cb 2.1.

605 **impetrabilior** (< *impetrabilis*): "more effective, efficacious."
qui uiuat: relative clause of characteristic depending on *nullus est* (AG 535a).

606 **Accherunti**: "in Acheron, in the underworld"; locative. See on 290.
nusquam gentium: "nowhere in the world."

607 **illaec**: modifies *oratio*.
interemit < *interimo*, "kill."

608 **quom rem agas**: "although you should be taking action"; concessive clause with *cum* (AG 549). There is prosodic hiatus after *rem*.
longinquom loqui: "to talk for long"; the infinitive is in apposition to *odiosast oratio*.

609 **ad capita rerum**: "to the heart of the matter."

611   **alienata est aps te**: i.e., Charinus has no more legal rights to the girl and therefore cannot sell her (see note on 449 and 457).
capital (sc. *facinus*): "capital offence," i.e., a crime punishable by death or loss of civil rights (*OLD capital* 1).
612   **aequalem** < *aequalis*, "of the same age."
613   **ne di sierint**: "God forbid!" (*sierint*= *siuerint*).
gladium: "sword."
iugulum: "neck."
cadam < *cado*, "fall."
614   **desponde** < *despondeo*, "give up, lose"; prohibition with *ne*.
quem despondeam: "which I could give up." The antecedent is *animum* in this relative clause of purpose.
615   **porro**: "then."
quoii= *cui*.
616   **addicta** < *addico*, "surrender, sell out" (*OLD addico* 6); the first syllable is shortened because of the accent on *iam*.
uenio: The historical present is used instead of the perfect in a *cum* temporal clause.
617   **montis tu quidem mali in me ardentis iam dudum iacis**: "for a long time you have certainly been piling upon me burning mountains of misery."
618   **perge** < *pergo*, "continue."
excrucia < *excrucio*, "torture."
carnufex: "executioner"; vocative.
quandoquidem: See on 171.
semel: "once."
625   **fidem mecum tuam**: For the expression see on 531.
626   **istanc**= *in istac re*, "in this situation."
non...ullam= *nullam*.
eugepae: "oh, great! good job!" This is an ironic Greek apostrophe.
627   **deos absentis testis memoras**: "you call upon the absent gods as witnesses."
qui ego istuc credam tibi: "how shall I believe those words of yours?" *credo* with an accusative of inner object (neuter pronoun) and a dative (indirect object). There is prosodic hiatus after *qui*.
628   **in manu est**: "is in (your) power; is up to you."

629	**argutus**: "bright, witty."
	par pari: "as equal to equal."
630	**ad mandata**: "in carrying out orders."
	claudus: "lame."
	caecus: "blind."
	mutus: "dumb, inarticulate."
	mancus: "crippled."
	debilis: "impotent."
632	**docto** < *doctus*, "expert."
	is lapidi mando maxumo: "I left the matter to the biggest stone (idiot)"; *is* is in apposition with *ego* in the previous line, emphasizing the personal pronoun, "I, he who."
633	**quid ego facerem**: direct question, with deliberative subjunctive.
	requireres: "you should have asked"; the four imperfect subjunctives in the next five lines (*requireres, rogitares, inuenires, exquireres*) are hortatory to express unfulfilled obligation in past time (AG 439b).
634	**prosapia**: "stock, family"; ablative of source (AG 403.2a).
635	**ciuisne esset an peregrinus**: double indirect question, depending on *rogitares*; *peregrinus*: "foreigner."
636	**saltem**: "at least."
638	**qua forma esse**: sc. *eum*= the buyer; *qua forma*, ablative of description.
639	**canum**: "grey-haired"; the accusatives in this line are used as predicates in the implied indirect statement *eum esse aiebant*. All adjectives form *homoioteleuton*.
	uarum: "knock-kneed, bow-legged."
	uentriosum: "pot-bellied."
	bucculentum: "big-mouthed."
	breuiculum: "short."
640	**subnigris** < *subniger*, "blackish"; ablative of description.
	oblongis malis: "with rather long (i.e., because of age) cheeks"; *malis* < *mala*, "cheek."
	pansam < *pansa*, "with splayed feet"; the adjective is masculine.
	aliquantulum: "just a little bit." The caricature description of an elderly man is a stock feature of Greek New Comedy

641	**thensaurum ... mali**: See on 163. **nescioquem**: "some."
642	**tantum**: "that's all." **quod sciam**: "so far as I know"; relative clause of characteristic expressing restriction (AG 535d).
643	**ne**: "indeed, surely"; affirmative particle. **oblongis malis...magnum malum**: Charinus puns on *māla* ("cheek") and *mălum* ("evil").
646	**Megares** (< *Megareus*): used in the plural as "the state of Megara." **Chalcidem**: Chalcis, a city in Euboea.
647	**Sicyonem**: Sicyon, a city in the Peloponnese. **Lesbiam**: Charinus uses the adjective *Lesbius* for the expected noun *Lesbos*; an homoioteleuton with *Boeotiam*. Charinus is thinking of all possible places in Greece to relocate, from Crete (south) and Cyprus (east) to Lesbos (northeast) and Zacynthos (west).
648	**istuc**: See on 165. **coeptas** < *coepio*, "venture on"; frequentative of *coepi*.
649	**quom illuc ... ueneris**: *cum* + future perfect in a temporal clause. **paritas** < *parito*, "arrange"; frequentative of *paro*.
650	**si ibi**: prosodic hiatus on *si*. **forte**: "by chance." **item**: "likewise." **inopia**: "need of, scarcity of"; + genitive (*eius*, i.e., of the person with whom you will fall in love).
651	**porro**: "forward, again."
652	**modus ... exsilio**: "end to (your) exile." Scan *ĕxsĭlĭō* with iambic shortening on the first syllable. **qui finis**: "what limit."
654	**cedo** (archaic imperative): "tell me, explain to me." **hac urbe**: ablative of separation after *abis*. **relicturum**: sc. *te esse*.
655	**fore**= *futurum esse*; the infinitive is the subject of *acceptumst*. **sat animo acceptumst**: "is fully accepted in your heart." **pro certo**: "for certain."

656	**quanto ... satiust**: "how much more preferable is it."
	aliquo: "somewhere"; adverbial ablative.
657	**adeo dum**: "for as long until"; + present indicative when there is no idea of expectancy (AG 553 n.2).
	illius: sc. *Pasicompsae*. Scan as bisyllabic, *īllī(u)s*.
	te ... missum facit: "discharges you." See on 84.
658	**dixti**= *dixisti*.
	hoc: sc. *exsulatum ... ire* (644).
660	**consili**: partitive genitive after *aliquid*. Charinus exits in despair, thinking that he has lost Pasicompsa forever.
661	**ut**: "how" (exclamatory).
	corripuit se: "he hurried over."
662	**mea ignauia**: ablative of cause.
663	**certumst praeconum iubere iam quantum est conducier**: "I have decided to order now as many criers as are (available) to be hired." *praeco* is a crier, who would make public announcements, possibly an auctioneer; *conducier*= *conduci*.
664	**inuestigent** < *inuestigo*, "trace."
	ad praetorem: The praetor had the power to give agents to a citizen (*conquaestores*: "detectives, inspectors"; they were like low-ranking police officers) to search for something lost, frequently a run-away slave.
665	**uicis** < *uicus*, "street."
666	**relicti**: partitive genitive with *quicquam*.

ACT IV SCENE i
Dorippa, Lysimachus' wife, returns from the country house, together with her slave Syra. Meter: Iambic Senarii. See Introduction, Meter Cb 1.1.

⌣ ⌣   ⁻│⌣   ⁻│⁻   ⁻│⁻   ⁻│⁻   ⁻│⌣ ⁻
quoni(am) a uir(o) ad me // rus aduenit nuntius

667	**quoniam**: "since."
	nuntius: "messenger."
668	**rus non iturum**: sc. *eum* (i.e., *Lysimachum*) *esse*.
	feci ego ingenium meum: "I made up my mind."
669	**qui me fugit**: The antecedent is *illum* (i.e., Lysimachus).
670	**anum** < *anus*, "old woman."
	consequi < *consequor*, "follow, come after."

670 **nostram Syram**: in apposition with *anum*.
671 **eccam**= *ecce illam*.
incedit: See 406. Syra's slow pace is due to her old age and the baggage she is carrying.
is (< *eo*): present indicative.
ocius: "faster"; (defective adverb, AG 130).
672 **mecastor**: "my Castor!" (see note on 6).
onerist= *oneris est*; < *onus*, "weight"; partitive genitive after *tantum*.
673 **octaginta et quattuor**: "eighty-four."
674 **eodem**: sc. *oneri*. Scan *eo-* as one syllable by synizesis.
accedit: "is added."
seruitus, sudor, sitis: "slavery, sweat, thirst." Notice the forceful alliteration.
675 **deprimunt** < *deprimo*, "weigh down."Dorippa sees the altar next to Demipho's house and wants to make an offering.
676 For the meaning of the daggers see on 17. The following emendation yields the most satisfactory meaning: *qui hanc uicini aram <Apollinis> nostri augeam*: "with which I may honor our neighbor's altar of Apollo."
677 **sane**: "if you will."
uirgam: "branch."
lauri < *laurus*, "laurel, bay tree."
eo: Syra goes into the house, sees Pasicompsa, and exits in horror in 681.
678 **pacem**: "blessing; benevolence" (*OLD pax* 2).
propitius: "as favorably, kindly disposed."
679 **sanitatem**: "sound health."
parcas < *parco*, "spare"; + dative.
681 **disperii**: See on 599.
682 **eiulas** < *eiulo*, "wail; lament."
683 **quid clamas**: Scan as *quĭd clāmās* (iambic shortening).
684 **nescioquaest**: "some"; modifies *mulier*. Scan as *nēscĭŏ-*.
685 **meretrix**: "prostitute."
ueron serio: "really and truly (seriously)."
686 **scis sapere**: "you are very wise."
ruri quae non manseris: "since you did not stay in the country"; relative clause of characteristic expressing cause.
687 **quamuis insipiens**: "even a fool."

persentiscere: "to realize, find out." After 687, there is a missing line from manuscript A; 687a is an attempt at reconstruction.

687a **temere**: "by chance."
mansisse (< *maneo*): The infinitive depends on *persentiscere*.
palamst: "it is obvious."

688 **bellissumi**: Syra is being sarcastic, since Lysimachus is an old man (see also on 812).

689 **ei**= *i*, present imperative of *eo*.
semul= *simul*.

690 **Alcumenam**= *Alcmenam*, the mother of Hercules. To the dismay of Juno she was impregnated by Jupiter, disguised as her own husband Amphitruo (cf. Plautus' own *Amphitruo*).
paelicem < *paelex*, "concubine."

691 **istuc eo quantum potest**: "I come to you, as fast as I can."

ACT IV SCENE ii
Lysimachus returns from the forum.
Meter: Iambic Senarii. See Introduction, Meter Cb 1,1.

⏑ ⏑ – | ⏑ ⏑ – – | – – ⏑ ⏑ | – – | – ⏑ –
parumne (e)st malai // rei quod amat Demipho

692 **parumne est malai rei, quod amat Demipho**: "is it not enough of a bad thing the fact that Demipho is in love?" For this use of *quod* see on 554; *malai*= *malae*. There is iambic shortening of *parum-*.

693 **ni sumptuosus insuper etiam siet**: "without his being too extravagant in addition." This is a negative stipulative clause (see on 146). In the fourth foot there is a *breuis in longo* on the ultima of *insuper*, resulting in a double short syllable instead of an iamb (see on 412).

694 **si uocasset** (= *uocauisset*): "even if he had invited"; iambic shortening on *decem*.
summos uiros: "very important men," i.e., of the upper class.

695 **nimium opsonauit**: "he bought too much food."

696 **hortator**: "the crier; the coxswain who gives orders to the oarsmen."
remiges: "rowers, oarsmen."
hortarier < *hortor*, "urge on"; + accusative.

698	**demiror**: "I wonder"; + accusative with infinitive (*eum ... non uenire*).
699	**quinam**: "who in the world."
	a nobis= *nostra domo*
	foris: "door"; nominative singular, subject of *aperitur*.

ACT IV SCENE iii
The discovery of Pasicompsa by Syra at Lysimachus' house results in a fight between Dorippa and her husband.
Meter: Iambic Senarii. See Introduction, Meter Cb 1.1.

⏑ ⏑ ⏑̄|‾ ⏑ ⏑|‾ ‾| ‾ ‾|‾ ‾ |⏑̆ ‾
miserior mulier // me nec fiet nec fuit

700	**me**: ablative of comparison.
701	**nupserim** < *nubo*, "get married to"; + dative. This is a relative clause of characteristic expressing cause.
	heu: an interjection usually followed by a dative of reference (AG 379a).
702	**quoi ... commendes uiro**: "to what man you could entrust"; *commendes* is a potential subjunctive, used for sarcasm.
	quae tu habeas: The subjunctive in the relative clause (antecedent is *tua*, "your possessions") is by attraction to *commendes* (see 36).
703	**decem talenta**: For the *talentum* see notes on 89 and 488.
	dotis < *dos*, "dowry."
	detuli < *defero*, "transfer." Marriage is based on the transferral of the wife's property to her husband's power (marriage by *manu*). The dowry, however, may be recoverable by the wife's family in the case of divorce. A *dotata uxor* is portrayed in comedy as having significant power over her husband because of her dowry and the threat of withdrawing it (see below 784-792). See S. Treggiari, *Roman Marriage: Iusti Coniuges from the Time of Cicero to the Time of Ulpian* (Oxford 1992).
704	**contumelias**: "insults."
706	**uidisse**: sc. *eam*, i.e., *uxorem meam* (subject).
707	**quae loquatur**: "what she is saying"; indirect question.
	exaudire: "to listen and understand."
708	**accedam** < *accedo*, "approach."

709	**oppido**: "completely."
710	**uidit**: Scan as *uīdīt*.
	ut te omnes ... di perduint: "would that all the gods would destroy you!"; *ut*= *utinam*, *perduint*= *perdiderint* (optative subjunctive).
711	**hoc est quod**: "this is the reason that"; causal *quod*.
712	**ego faciam**: Scan as *ĕgŏ făcĭăm*, iambic shortening of *ego*.
	nisi uti: "except to"; prosodic hiatus after *uti* (bisyllabic iambic word).
	adeam < *adeo*, "approach."
713	**iubet saluere suo' uir uxorem suam**: This is a very formal address between a husband and wife with a grandiose tone.
714	**urbani fiunt rustici**: "are the country folk becoming city folk?" i.e., "do those who live in the country come to the city?"
	pudicius < *pudice*, "with a greater sense of propriety"; comparative adverb.
715	**quam illi**: There is hiatus between the two words for emphasis on the message Dorippa wants to convey.
716	**delinquont** < *delinquo*, "misbehave." Lysimachus pretends to have understood that the country houseslaves have inappropriately treated Dorippa, who came to the city to seek her husband's help.
717	**multo minu' mali**: "much less trouble."
721	**temptas** < *tempto*, "tease."
719	**quoia**: "whose."
720	**quoia ea sit**: indirect question, depending on *rogitas*. Lysimachus repeats the same questions again and again to avoid giving a straight answer.
723	**haeres** < *haereo*, "hesitate, be stuck."
	hau uidi magis: sc. *aliquem haerentem*.
724	**quin si liceat**: sc. *dicam*, "in fact, if I may, I shall say..."
	dictum oportuit: "you ought to have said already"; *oportet* + accusative of perfect passive participle (a colloquial construction).
725	**ita instas**: "the way you insist."
	urges quasi pro noxio: "you push me, as if I were guilty of a crime."

726 **innoxiu's**: "you are innocent." Dorippa is being ironic; scan with iambic shortening: *scĭ(o) ĭnnōxĭū's*.
(sc. *tam*) **audacter quamuis dicito**: "say it with as much assurance as you wish."

727 **atqui**: The conjunction expresses strong threat or threatening action (Lindsay, *Syntax* VIII.2).
dicundum est: "it must be said."

728 **nihil agis**: See on 459.

729 **manufesto**: "in the act; red-handed."
teneo in noxia: "I catch you in guilt."

730 **istaquidem**: i.e., *ista puella*.
†**iohia**†: This is another *locus desperatus*; see on 17. We should assume that Dorippa keeps asking whose the girl is.

731 **si nihil usus esset**: "unless there were some need"; contrary-to-fact present condition.

732-35 The numbering here as elsewhere reflects the traditional ordering in the manuscripts.

736 **sum iudex captus**: "I have been appointed as an arbitrator"; *iudex* is a predicate nominative.

737 **tu in consilium istam aduocauisti tibi**: "you have summoned her for consultation with you." An arbitrator (*iudex*) would normally summon his friends for consultation (*aduocare*) concerning the matter in dispute, in this case the girl. Dorippa is making fun of Lysimachus' lame story: was he seeking assistance from the girl who is the very subject of the arbitration?

738 **immo sic**: Scan as *ĭmmŏ sīc* (*immo* as a pyrrhic is unusual).
sequestro < *sequester*, "trustee"; modifies *mihi*. A *sequester* is the third party in an altercation to whom disputed property is entrusted to await the result of the dispute: property could be something valuable or even a slave (in this case, Pasicompsa).

739 **istius**: "of the sort of thing you have in mind." Lysimachus feels contempt for any immoral behavior, especially fornication.
numero: "too soon, too quickly."
purigas (< *pur(i)go*): "you attempt to exonerate yourself"; conative present (AG 467).

740 **negoti**: "trouble"; partitive genitive after *nimium*.

repperi < *reperio*, "meet with, hit upon."

ACT IV SCENE iv
The cook arrives with his assistants (who remain mute, carrying the groceries), only to make things worse between Lysimachus and Dorippa. The presence of a cook on stage is frequently employed by Greek and Roman playwrights, especially Plautus (see E. Gowers, *The Loaded Table. Representations of Food in Latin Literature*, Oxford 1993). Meter: Iambic Senarii. See Introduction, Meter Cb 1.1

```
 ˘ ˘  ⁻|  ⁻  ⁻|⁻   ⁻  |  ˘  ⁻|⁻  ⁻|˘ ˘
```
agit(e) it(e) actutum // nam m(i) amatori seni

741   **mi**: dative of agent after *coquendast* (see on 171).
      amatori seni: dative of advantage.
743   **nobis**: dative of reference (AG 376).
      non <quoi cond>ucti sumus: "for him by whom we have been hired." Stereotypically, slaves, such as the cook and his attendants, crave food and would do anything to obtain even very little.
744   **pro cibo**: "instead of food." The cook is philosophizing, as is usual for slaves or secondary characters in comedy (cf. Syra's monologue at the end of Act IV); prosodic hiatus after *qui* and *si*.
745   **uidere, amplecti, osculari, adloqui**: The infinitives are in apposition with the previous line (see 608), explaining how someone in love reacts; the point is that lovers do not long for food but rather for the object of their affection (*amplecti*: see on 570; *osculari*: see on 571).
746   **sed nos confido onustos redituros domum**: "but I trust we will return home loaded (with food)"; *onustos* is a predicate adjective agreeing with *nos* (accusative with infinitive in indirect statement).
747   **eite**= *ite*. See Introduction, Language B 2j.
749   **st**: "hush!" Scan as a long syllable.
      abei= *abi* (second person singular present imperative).
750   **non estis cenaturi**: "you are not going to dine?"
      saturi: "full, stuffed."

751	**sed— interii**: This is an unusual place for iambic shortening (on *in-*) with the change of speakers; scan as *sĕd ĭntĕrĭī*. *sed* is perhaps a miswriting for *st*.
	illi: antecedent of the relative clause *quos inter iudex datu's*.
752	**quos inter**: anastrophe of the preposition.
	iudex: See on 736.
754	**dixtei**= *dixisti*. We can imagine that when Lysimachus hired the cook he claimed that the girl was his own and not Demipho's, either because he was also enchanted by Pasicompsa's beauty (see 518-519) or simply because he was trying to cover his friend's tracks.
	opsonabas: "you were purchasing the food."
755	**scitum** < *scitus*, "handsome, nice."
	filum mulieris: "texture, quality, style, figure of a woman"; loaded with sexual innuendo.
	anet: "she is an old woman"; cf. *anus* in 670.
756	**abin dierectus**: "go to hell!"; scan with iambic shortening: *ăbĭn dĭērēctŭs*.
758	**quid est**: "what!" (with indignation).
760	**nempe**: "surely; of course."
	quam: The antecedent is *uxor*.
761	**atque anguis**: "just as (you hate) snakes"; for this use of *atque* see AG 324c.
762	**mihi quidem**: The emphasis falls on *mihi*, therefore scan as *mĭhī quĭd(em)*.
	ita me amabit Jupiter: "for the love of Jupiter!" "so help me Heaven!"
763	**ut ego illud numquam deixi**: "as I have never said this!"
764	**palam istaec fiunt**: "the situation becomes clearly obvious"; the accusative with infinitive *te ... odisse* is in apposition with this expression.
	quin nego: "in fact, I deny it."
765	**ted**= *te*.
	aibat= *aiebat*.
766	Notice the iambic shortening of *ĕt ŭxōrēm* and the synizesis of *suam*.
767	**molestu's**: "you are harassing."
768	**sapio**: sc. *si illam metuo*.

769   **experirei**= *experiri* (< *experior*, "try"); the verb here implies possibly taking the matter to court and having both the cook and Lysimachus cross-examined (*me* is the object of the infinitive).
    mercedem < *merces*, "payment, salary."
    cedo: See on 149.
771   **experior**: "I am learning by experience" (*OLD experior* 4b).
    uetus: modifies *uerbum*.
772   **aliquid mali esse propter uicinum malum**: "because of a bad neighbor, there is some trouble." Plautus alludes to Hesiod's similar proverb in *Works and Days* 346.
773   The verse ending with †*incommodi*† is metrically corrupt; (< *incommodum*, "disadvantage, detriment").
774   Iambic shortening of *e-* in *ĕuēnīt*.
775   **eradicas** < *eradico*, "annihilate, finish off."
776   **abibitur**: "I will depart"; *eo* can be often found in the passive voice.
777   **drachmam**: The amount the cook asks is insignificant.
    darei= *dari*.
    sis= *si uis*.
778   **darei**: Scan as *dārĕĭ* (iambic shortening because of the accent on the first syllable of *potest*).
    dum illei ponunt: sc. *opsonia*, "while they are putting down the groceries."
779   **ut molestus ne sis**: "can't you stop harassing me?"; negative substantive purpose clause after *potine* (see on 441).
    apponite < *appono*, "put x (accusative) down next to y (dative)"; here with *opsonium istuc illi seni*.
781   **uassa**= *uasa*, "dishes, baskets"; plural of *uas*.
782   **sequimini**: second person plural present imperative of the deponent *sequor*. Scan with iambic shortening on the ultimate because of the accent on the penultimate *sĕquĭmĭnĭ*. The first foot then has an unusual proceleusmatic.
    fortasse: "perhaps." Here as often in Plautus, it is constructed with an accusative and infinitive (*OLD fortasse* f).
783   **quod uenit et haec attulit**: causal clauses; *attulit* < *affero*.
784   **damni facis aut flagiti**: See on 237 for the expression; *miror* is often followed by a *si*-clause in the indicative (AG 572b note).

785	**seic**= *sic*; *me nuptam* sc. *esse*.
786	**scorta** < *scortum*, "prostitute."
	obductarier= *obductari* (< *obducto*): "to bring in, introduce into one's presence."
787	**uerbeis meeis**: "in my name; on my behalf." Dorippa now threatens Lysimachus with divorce. In comedy, women can initiate the process for divorce, especially the *uxores dotatae* (see on 703 above), a right that otherwise only men could exercise. Such resolution would be admissible to women who married *sine manu*, i.e., without transferring their father's power over to their husband.
788	**tecum**: Scan *tēcŭm*.
790	**concepteis uerbeis**: "in formal language, with a formal contract." Lysimachus claims he can assure Dorippa through a formal contract (*stipulatio* or *sponsio*) that he has not been cheating on her.
	iusiurandum dabo: "I shall take an oath."
791	Lysimachus leaves his oath unfinished, since Syra is already on her way to his father-in-law.
793	**perduint**=*perdiderint*.
794	**tua**: Scan with synizesis.
	amationibus < *amatio*, "love affair."
795	**suspicione impleuit me indignissume**: "he filled me up with suspicion most undeservedly"; *impleo* + ablative of means.
796	**conciuit** < *concieo* or *concio*, "summon."
	hostis: accusative plural; object of *conciuit*.
	acerrumast < *acer*, "is most ferocious".
798	**istanc**: sc. *Pasicompsam*.
	capillo < *capillus*, "hair"; ablative of means.
	protracturum < *protraho*, "drag"; infinitive in indirect statement after *eloquar*, the apodosis of the future-more-vivid condition of the next line.
799	**abducit**: present tense with future force.
	quo volt: "to whatever place he wishes."
800	**quamquam**: "although."
801	**auferrier**= *auferri* (< *aufero*) "to be carried away."
802	**eadem**: sc. *opera*, "by the same effort; at the same time." Scan with synizesis on *ea-*.
	rectius: "rather properly" (*OLD recte* 4).

ACT IV SCENE v
Syra returns from Dorippa's father's house, while Eutychus returns after having searched the whole city to find Pasicompsa. Meter: Iambic Senarii. See Introduction, Meter Cb 1.1.

⏑ ⏑ ‒ | ‒ ‒ | ‒ ‒ | ⏑ ‒ | ‒ ‒ | ⏑ ‒

era quo me misit // ad patrem non est domi

803 **ad patrem**: in apposition with *quo*; the syntax, however, does not follow, since Syra is probably panting and therefore uses a colloquialism. Understand: *pater, quo me misit, non est domi.*
805 **defessus**: "exhausted."
peruenarier= *peruenari* (< *peruenor*): "to hunt, search thoroughly."
806 **inuestigo**: "discover."
809 **alumnus**: "nursling."
tuo'= *tuus.*
alumnule: Syra uses the diminutive here as a display of affection for Eutychus, whom she has reared all these years.
811 **familiai**= *familiae.*
812 **pater bellissumus**: ironic (see also on 688); iambic shortening of *istuc.*
813 **quo modo**: "how can it be?" (with indignation).
814 **offendit** < *offendo*, "come upon."
815 **istarum operarum**: "of that sort," literally, "of those deeds you describe"; genitive of quality (AG 345). The adjectival pronoun *istarum* is used in a pejorative sense, to describe Lysimachus' affair with Pasicompsa, which Eutychus finds hard to believe.

ACT IV SCENE vi
Syra asks for a transformation of the legal system, which has been discriminating against women. Sexual licentiousness should be a cause of divorce for a respectable Roman matrona. Meter: Iambic Senarii. See Introduction, Meter Cb 1.1.

‒ ‒ | ‒ ⏑ | ‒ ⏑ | ‒ | ‒ ‒ | ⏑ ⏑ | ‒

ecastor lege // dura uiuont mulieres

818	**multo iniquiore**: sc. *lege*, "under much unfairer conditions"; *multo* is an ablative of degree of difference.
819	**duxit**: The verb applies to men when they get married (*uxorem ducere*, as opposed to *nubere*, see on 701) and is sarcastically applied to men taking prostitutes into their houses. In 819-822, *si duxit, si resciuit, si egressa est* are present general conditions (indefinite time, AG 518b).
820	**inpunest uiro**: "the husband goes unpunished"; *uiro* is a dative of advantage.
821	**foras**: A wife needs her husband's permission to go out.
822	**uiro fit caussa**: "an excuse is created for the husband," "it becomes an excuse for the husband." **exigitur matrumonio**: "she is driven from the marriage," "she is divorced." This formula is taken from legal terminology: after the divorce, women must leave their husband's house.
823	**utinam lex esset eadem quae uxori est uiro**: "would that the same law that applies to women applied to men!" Syra's wish is incapable of fulfillment, as the imperfect subjunctive indicates (AG 441).
824	This is a reflection of the ideal of the *uniuira uxor*, the Roman woman who is the wife of one husband.
825	**qui**= *quo*, "why?"
826	**faxim**= *fecerim*, "I guarantee that"; the optative *faxim* is followed by a substantive clause of result without *ut*. **itidem**: "just as" (with *ut* in 828). **plectantur** < *plecto*, "punish."
828	**ut illae exiguntur**: Scan with iambic shortening on *ĭll(ae)*. **culpam commerent**: "are guilty of the offence (sc. of adultery)."
829	**uidui** < *uiduus*, "spouseless."
826-29	"By Castor, I guarantee that if men were punished in the same way (if anyone took a prostitute without his wife's knowledge) that women guilty of adultery are divorced, there would be more spouseless men than women."

ACT V SCENE i
Charinus comes out of his father's house, all packed and ready to sail off; this is the only viable way to overcome his love for Pasicompsa.

Plautus *Mercator*

Meter: Trochaic Septenarii. See Introduction, Meter Cb 2.1.

```
  ‒  ‒ | ‒  ⌣ ‒ |       ‒  ‒| ‒    ⌣ | ‒   ‒| ⌣  ⌣  ‒| ‒     ⌣| ‒
```
limen superum<qu(e)> inferumque :: salue simul autem uale

830 **limen superum<que> inferumque:** "upper and lower threshold" (vocative). Notice Charinus' comic and yet very solemn farewell to the threshold of his father's house. The *limen* is protected by its tutelary god *Limentarius*. Charinus' despair becomes madness in the second scene; it will, however, soon give way to a happy ending by the end of the act. Charinus' tragic monologue alludes to similar farewell speeches from tragedy, possibly parodying Pacuvius' *Teucer* (Ajax's brother, exiled to Cyprus). Livius Andronicus also wrote a tragedy *Teucer*, while Ennius wrote a similar play called *Telamon*.

831 **hunc ... postremum ... pedem:** The words have been chosen for dramatic effect.
patria: "ancestral"; modifies *domo*.

832 **usus, fructus:** "the right both to use another's property and to receive profits from it" (*OLD usus* 4b).
uictus: "sustenance."
cultus: "personal care and maintenance" (*OLD cultus* 4). Notice the separate placement of nouns in 832 and of their modifying verbs in 833.
harunc: *harum + ce*.

833 **interemptust:** "has been destroyed."
interfectust < *interficio*, "kill, annihilate."
alienatust < *alieno*, "give up, lose."
occidi < *occido*, "die, perish."

834 **meum parentum**= *meorum parentorum* (syncopated genitive).
familiai Lar Pater: Each house has its own household gods, the *Lares* and *Penates*. The *Penates* are specifically guarding the master of the house and his kindred, whereas the *Lares* protect all indiscriminately.

835 **tutemini** < *tutor*, "protect, defend"; jussive clause (substantive clause of purpose) after *mando*.

836 **penatis:** accusative plural.

837 **abhorreo:** "I shrink back from"; + *ab* with ablative.

Plautus *Mercator*

838 **ubi**: introduces a relative clause (antecedent is *Atticis*); prosodic hiatus after *nam*.
deteriores: "worse"; predicate nominative to *mores* (< *mos*, see on 513).
increbrescunt < *increbresco*, "increase, rise."
in dies: "day by day."

839 **qui amici, qui infideles sint**: indirect questions depending on *pernoscere*, "to examine and distinguish."

840 **ubique id eripiatur, animo tuo quod placeat maxume**: "and where what most pleases your heart, shall be taken away from you."

841 **si**: "even though"; concessive *si* with subjunctive (AG 527c n.2).

ACT V SCENE ii
Eutychus will try one more time to dissuade Charinus from pursuing voluntary exile. Meter: Trochaic Septenarii. See Introduction, Meter Cb 2.1.

$$\bar{\ }\quad\bar{\ }\ |\quad\smile\smile\bar{\ }\ |\quad\bar{\ }\quad\bar{\ }\ |\bar{\smile}\bar{\ }\ |$$
diu(om) atqu(e) hominum quae spectatrix ::

$$\bar{\ }\quad\bar{\smile}|\quad\bar{\ }\ \bar{\ }\ |\quad\smile\smile\smile|\bar{\ }$$
atqu(e) er(a) eadem (e)s hominibus

842 By sharp contrast to Charinus' farewell lamentation, Eurychus delivers a thanksgiving hymn to the goddess Fortuna.
diuom= *deum*, genitive plural.
spectatrix: "observer; scrutinizer"; scan *ea-* as one syllable by synizesis.

843 **spem**: "fulfillment of hope" (Enk 170). Notice the alliteration: *spem speratam*, and in the following line: *laetus laetitia*.
obtulisti < *offero*, "present, offer."

844 **ecquisnam**: "any."
fuat= *sit* (present subjunctive from the root of the perfect tense); relative clause of characteristic (AG 535a).

845 **domi erat**: Scan as *dŏmĭ ĕrāt* (emphatic iambic words, like *domi* here, are left in prosodic hiatus).

quaeritabam < *quaerito*, "search"; frequentative of *quaero*.
sex: "six."
sodalis= *sodales*.

846 **uitam, amicitiam, ciuitatem**: I.e., he has saved Charinus' life, he has restored the almost lost trust between the two friends, and he will prevent Charinus' departure from their city. Scan ămĭcĭtĭām with iambic shortening.
ludum, iocum: "play and sport."

847 **eorum inuentu**: "by finding those (i.e., six companions)." The ablative of the supine, *inuentu*, is used here as an ablative of means.
res ... pessumas pessum dedi: "I sent to the bottom; I put an end to the worst of evils."
simitu= *simul*.

848 **maerorem** < *maeror*, "sadness."

849 **exitium**: "destruction."
pertinaciam: "stubbornness." This line has been considered an interpolation, because in 846 Eutychus speaks of six newly found advantages, whereas in 848-849 he lists ten habits of his past life that he now foregoes. However, there need not be a match between the six virtues and the number of vices. After 849, a *lacuna*, i.e., a gap in the text, has been detected. In the missing line, Eutychus would state that he has been looking for Charinus.

850 **conueniundi ... eius ... copiam**: "the opportunity of meeting him"; *conveniundi* < *conuenio*, here in the genitive with *copiam*.

851 **apparatus**: "equipped."
ut uidetis: "as you see."
abicio: "I put aside."
superbiam: "pride"; i.e., his life-style, since he was used to having slaves, companions for the road, a horse.

852 **calator**: "personal attendant; footman."
equos= *equus*.
agaso: "stable boy; groom."
armiger: "armor-bearer; squire."

853 **imperator**: "commander."
idem egomet: "I myself."
oboedio: "I listen to, obey"; + dative.

854	**usust**= *usui est*, "is useful."
	quantus es!: "how much power you have!"
855	**quemuis**: "whomever you please."
	facile ... factis facis: alliteration.
856	**eundem**: sc. *facis*.
	diffidentem: "distrusting, hopeless."
	denuo: "anew."
857	**quonam**: "where in the world"; *quonam curram*: indirect question depending on *cogito*.
	illum... quaeritatum: "to look for him"; supine of purpose.
	certa res (sc. *mihi est*): "the thing is decided," i.e., "I have decided"; + infinitive.
858	**usque**: "without an interruption."
	quoquo hinc abductast gentium: "to wherever in the world she has been taken from here."
859	**opsistet** < *obsisto*, "stand in the way."
	amnis: "river"; *ulla* modifies *amnis*, which is feminine in archaic but masculine in classical Latin.
	neque adeo: "not even."
860	**calor**: "heat." The noun is irregularly neuter here, but elsewhere it is masculine.
	frigus: "cold", neuter.
	grandinem < *grando*, "hail."
861	**imbrem** < *imber*, "rain."
	perpetiar < *perpetior*, "suffer, endure."
	sufferam < *suffero*, "put up with."
862	**concedam** < *concedo*, "give up."
	dius: "by day; during the day" (adverbial accusative of duration of time).
863	**aut amicam aut mortem inuestigauero**: *inuestigauero* has by *zeugma* two objects, whereas for *mortem* we could expect a verb like *inuenero*.
864	**nescioquoia**= *nescio* + *cuius*: "somebody's."
	auris: "ears."
	aduolauit < *aduolo*, "fly to, reach."
	inuoco: For the second time, Charinus delivers a farewell to his home and country.
865	**Lares uiales**: "Lares of the roadsides." The cult of the *Lares* was possibly imported into the household from their worship

in the fields and the *compita*, the crossroads. In this instance, the *Lares uiales* protect the travelers by guarding the roads.
tutetis < *tuto*, "protect."

866   Iambic shortening of *bene*.

867   **sta**: second person singular present active imperative.

868   Charinus believes that the three personified goddesses (*Spes, Salus, Victoria*) have just called on him.
comitem: predicate accusative to *alium* after *quaerite*.

869   **amittunt**= *demittunt* < *demitto*, "let go." Charinus explains in 870 who those companions are. Scan the final *ei* as bisyllabic, *ĕī*.

871   **repudia** < *repudio*, "renounce, scorn"; present imperative.
respice < *respicio*, "look back"; + accusative.
reuortere: imperative of *reuertor*, "come back."

872   **supsequere** < *subsequor*, "follow behind"; present imperative; the first syllable of *siquidem* is short by *enclisis* (see on 171).

887   This emended verse makes better sense if placed after 872, although †*sta ilico*† remains a problemàtic repetition; an iamb is allowed in the fourth foot of the septenarius, *amic(o)*, at the *diaeresis*.
multum beneuolens: "with much good-will."

873   **commorare**= *commoraris* (< *commoror*): "you delay."
sol abit: "The sun is setting."

874   **si huc item properes ut istuc properas, facias rectius**: "if you would hurry over here in the same way you are hurrying over there, you would do better."

875   **secundus uentus**: "favorable wind."
uorsoriam (sc. *funem*) < *uersoria*, the rope used to set the sail at an angle (in order to catch favorable wind); *uorsoriam capere*: "to turn the direction of the ship (expecting to find calmer seas); to tack about."

876   **fauonius**: "west wind."
auster: "east wind."
imbricus: "rainy." The east wind brings rain and storms (Charinus' exile eastward), whereas the western breeze is always pleasant (the place where Eutychus stands).

877   **omnis**: accusative plural; modifies *fluctus*, "storms."

conciet: "stirs up." Eutychus uses nautical language to dissuade Charinus from pursuing his plans. He claims that Charinus' decision is like running headlong towards a storm.

878 **recipe te ad terram**: "make for the land." In his distraught mind, Charinus has already sailed off; Eutychus has to bring him back to the shore (and to reality).
nonne: anticipates a positive answer.
ex aduorso: "from the opposite, unfavorable side."

879 **nubis**: "cloud"; modified by *atra* ("black").
<ut> instat: "how it presses on"; *ut* introduces indirect questions (879 and 880) with an indicative (see on 169).
sinisteram: The left side is the favorable one in Roman augury (cf. *Aeneid* 9.630).

880 **splendore**: ablative with *plenum* (elsewhere the adjective is followed by a genitive).
istuc: "to this place."
uorti= *reuorti*, "to return."

881 **religionem ... obiecit** < *religionem obicere*, "to bring forward a matter of religious scruple as a hindrance or disincentive to some action" (*OLD obicio* 9a).

882 **contra pariter fer gradum et confer pedem**: "move your feet towards me and march!" Eutychus uses formal language, alluding perhaps to tragedy (see note on 830), since Charinus has to return carefully and according to the ritual in order for the omen to be fulfilled.

883 **porge** < *porgo* or *porrigo*, "stretch out."
bracchium: "arm."
prehende: sc. *bracchium meum*.

884 **st!**: See on 749; here, however, it is used as an exclamation, outside the septenarius (*extra metrum*).

885 **ne paue**: "fear not!"
restituam < *restituo*, "restore."
in gaudio antiquo: "in your former joy."

886 **quod gaudeas**: "at which you may rejoice"; *gaudeo* with a neuter pronoun here (*OLD gaudeo* 1f). Notice the alliteration: *audire audies gaudeas*.

888 **tuam amicam**: See note on 181 for scansion. Eutychus does not finish his sentence because Charinus interrupts him.

889 **mauelim**: sc. *scire*.

890 **potin ut animo sis tranquillo**: "are you able to calm down?"; substantive clause of purpose after *potin*.
quid si mi animus fluctuat: "but what if my mind rages like a storm?"
891 **istum**: sc. *animum*.
in tranquillo quieto tuto: sc. *loco*. The adjectives form an asyndeton.
sistam < *sisto*, "place, fix."
892 **<propere>**: "quickly."
893 **reticentia**: "silence"; ablative of cause or means.
894 **commostras** < *commo(n)stro*, "show."
895 **modo**: "just now."
896 **EV. faciam. CH. longum istuc amantist**: EV. "I will make (you see her)." CH. "That "will" of yours is a long time for someone in love"; *amanti* is a dative of reference.
897 **atque is est**: "than he is." For the use of *atque* after words of comparison (*amicior*), see AG 324c.
898 **neque est quoi magi' me melius uelle aequom siet**: "nor is there (i.e., anyone else), for whom it would be fairer for me to wish all the best"; *quoi ... siet*: relative clause of characteristic (with subjunctive) after the negative *neque est* (AG 535a). Eutychus is referring to his father.
899 **istunc**: "the one you mention"; accusative object of *curo* (person affected).
901 **aedibus**: Scan as *aedibūs* with a long ultimate and *ĭll(a)* with iambic shortening (accent on *ubi*).
aedis probas: sc. *esse*; *aedis*: accusative plural, *probas*: "well-made," predicate accusative to *aedis*.
902 **aedificatas** < *aedifico*, "construct"; modifies *aedis*. As is common in comedy for people in love, Charinus immediately changes mood and, with different eyes, begins to appreciate how beautiful his neighbor's house is, since Pasicompsa has been there all this time.
arbitro: "I believe"; usually deponent (*arbitror*).
903 **quid**: "why?" Another change of mood, since Charinus immediately doubts that Eutychus has been speaking the truth; iambic shortening of *ĭstūc*.
de audito: "on hearsay" (Lindsay, *Syntax* VII.2).

Plautus *Mercator*

904	**quis eam adduxit ad uos**: Charinus implies that perhaps Eutychus was the person to whom his father wanted to sell the girl. **inque**: "say, speak"; imperative of *inquam*.
905	**nil ... te quidem quicquam pudet**: "then you are not ashamed of anything"; *pudet* is impersonal.
906	**quid tua refert**: "why does it matter to you?" (AG 355a). **dum**: "provided that"; proviso clause. **istic**: "in that place of yours."
907	**ob**: "on account of"; + accusative. **nuntium**: "message."
908	**ut eius faciant copiam**: "to provide an abundance of it (i.e., whatever you ask for)"; jussive clause depending on *orato*.
909	**derides** < *derideo*, "make fun." **seruata res est**: "the situation has been saved; all is well." **demum**: "then, finally."
910	**quin ornatum hunc reicio**: "why don't I get rid of all this stuff?" At the beginning of Act V Charinus was loaded up and ready for a long trip. Now that he has decided to stay, he needs to change clothes.
910-11	**aliquis ... exite**: For the syntax see on 131.
911	**pallium**: "mantle, cloak"; a metatheatrical jest in which Charinus gives up his tragic role and asks for a *pallium*, a cloak appropriate for comedy (cf. *palliata*, Introduction A). **ecferte** < *ecfero*, "bring out."
912	**puere**: archaic vocative addressed to the slave who now comes out of the house. **cape**: imperative of *capio*. **chlamydem** < *chlamys*, "woolen garment" (suitable for trips, worn by travellers and soldiers).
913	**si haec non sint uera**: The mood of the conditional clause (*sint*) is attracted to the subjunctive of the purpose clause (*ut ... exsequar*). **inceptum**: "begun." **itiner**: archaic accusative of *iter*, "journey." **perficere** < *perficio*, "finish, complete."
915	**paullisper**: "a little while."
916	**eundi**: genitive of the gerund depending on *tempus*, "time to go."

917	**non opus est**: here with an infinitive subject.
918	**qua caussa**: "why?"
	operae non est: "there is no spare time" (see on 14).
	commodum: "convenient."
	illi: sc. *Pasicompsae*.
919	**itane**: "is that so?"
	contra: "in return."
920	**omnibus hic**: The ultima of *omnibus* (*breuis in longo*) with *hic* forms an iamb as the second foot (see on 412). *omnibus ... modis*: "in every way possible."
	ludificatur < *ludificor*, "mock." Charinus still finds it hard to believe that Eutychus has actually found Pasicompsa.
921	**qui isti credam**: "since I trust that man"; *isti*: dative with *credam*.
	sumam < *sumo*, "take up, put on."
	denuo: "anew."
922	**parumper**: "a little while." Charinus takes off his *pallium* and puts on his travelling *chlamys* again.
923-24	**quia ... / ... adduxerit**: "because (as she thinks) he has brought in"; the subjunctive in the causal clause is used to indicate that the reason is that imagined by the mother, not one vouched for by the speaker (AG 540).
	ob oculos: "before her eyes."
	dum ... abest: For the tense and mood see on 193.
925	**suspicatur**: See on 215.
	illi: sc. *patri meo*, dative of reference.
	zonam: "belt, pouch"; used for keeping traveling money.
	sustuli < *tollo*, "take up." Charinus has now put on his belt and threatens Eutychus with immediate departure.
926	**machaera**: "knife; a short single-edged sword."
927	**ampullam**: "flask"; used for holding oil or other liquids. The Greeks and Romans used to rub their feet with oil before they put on their sandals.
928	**decipere**: "to deceive, dupe."
929	Because of the accent on *quin* and *me* there is iambic shortening on *ergo* and *meum*.
931	**currum** < *currus*, "chariot"; prosodic hiatus of the initial *iam*.
	escendi < *escendo*, "mount."

Plautus *Mercator*

931 **lora**: "reins."
932 **quin, pedes, uos in curriculum conicitis**: "my feet, why don't you throw yourselves into running"; the force of *quin* is "why ... not" as often.
933 **in Cyprum**: Charinus' first stop, like Teucer's, is in Cyprus (see note on 830).
recta (sc. *uia*): "on a straight course, directly."
934 **noli ... dicere**: "don't say"; prohibition (AG 450); scan *dīcĕrē* either with a lengthened final syllable or as *breuis in longo*.
935 **operam ut sumam**: "that I shall take up the task."
ad peruestigandum: "to investigate thoroughly"; accusative of the gerund expressing purpose (AG 506).
quin: "in fact."
936 **mentitust** < *mentior*, "lie"; + accusative (*id*).
937 **expetis**: "you are looking for."
938 **percontatus**: "though I investigated," < *percontor*; here a concessive participle.
matris iam iram neglego: Eutychus does not have any more reservations about leading Charinus into his house to see Pasicompsa. He can even put up with his mother's wrath, as long as he can help his "ailing" friend.
939 **quaesitum**: "to seek to find (her)"; supine of purpose. In his hallucinations Charinus explores all the places he may visit soon in search of Pasicompsa. In this imaginary trip of the mind he has already been in Cyprus and now he is moving to the town of Chalcis in Euboea. This scene possibly alludes to Euripides' *Herakles* (922-1015) where the hero suffers from similar delirium (a play perhaps already satirized in the Greek original by Philemon).
Chalcidem: accusative of place to which.
940 **Zacyntho**: ablative of source (see 634). Zacynthus, an island in the Ionian sea, was captured by the Romans in 211/210 and again in 191 BCE.
eo: "to this place."
941 **rogito**: "I keep asking"; with an indirect question introduced by *si*, "whether" (AG 576a).
uexerit < *ueho*, "carry."
indaudiuerit < *indaudio*, "hear as a rumor."

942	**omittis** < *omitto*, "lay aside, drop."
943	**Zacynthi**: locative (AG 427).
	ficos (<*ficus*, f.): "fig." The word is used by Aristophanes for the female genitalia (*Peace* 1360). The reference is perhaps adapted from Philemon's play or is part of the slang vocabulary of those soldiers who came back from Zacynthus.
	non malas: litotes, i.e., *pulchras*.
944	**autumat** (< *autumo*): "affirm, aver."
945	**Calchas**: predicate nominative to *iste ... Zacynthiust*. Calchas is the famous seer of the Trojan war. Eutychus mocks Charinus' tragic style.
946	The mental play continues: in his imaginary trip Charinus now leaves Chalcis to come back to Athens where his girlfriend is, according to his friend from Zacynthus.
	conscendo: "I embark."
948	**ut ualuisti**: "how have you been?"
949	**bene uocas, benigne dicis**: "it is nice of you to invite me to dinner, you are very kind." The expression is used to decline politely the invitation.
	cras apud te, nunc domi: "tomorrow (we will dine) at your house, now at mine."
950	**oportet**: "it ought to, it should."
	heia: "come now!" (used for ironic surprise, condescending); scan as *hĕiă*.
	quae mi somnias: "what dreams you have fabricated for me!"
951	**medicari** < *medicor*, "heal, cure"; + dative of person.
952	**clementer**: "gently."
	calces deteris: "you walk on my heels."
953	**componi** < *compono*, "arrange" (present passive infinitive).
955	**ergo cura**: "therefore, take care (to calm my mother down)."
956	**propitiam**: "gracious." Juno, famous for her jealousy, is never gracious to or forgiving of her husband, Jupiter.

ACT V SCENE iii
Demipho and Lysimachus return from the forum.
Meter: Trochaic Septenarii. See Introduction, Meter Cb 2.1.

˘ ˘ − | −   − | −   − | ˘ ˘ ˘ | −   − | − − | − ˘|−

quasi tu numquam quicqu(am) adsimile :: huiius facti feceris

Plautus *Mercator*

957 **quasi ... feceris**: clause of conditional comparison (see on 205). Demipho and Lysimachus have been fighting, while Demipho is trying to explain to his neighbor that it is normal for an old man to go astray once in a while.
adsimile: "similar"; + genitive (usually found with a dative). Scan *hui-* as one syllable by synizesis.

958 **caui**: "I took care"; + negative substantive clause of purpose (*ne ... facerem*).

959 **in fermento** < *fermentum*, "ferment." The expression refers to Dorippa's anger, which is compared to fermenting wine or to boiling food in general.

960 **expurigationem habebo**: "I will clean the matter up."
suscenseat < *suscenseo*, "be angry"; + dative of person.

ACT V SCENE iv
Eutychus comes out of the house. As the play is coming to an end, certain stipulations are imposed on Demipho by his neighbors.

Meter: Trochaic Septenarii. See Introduction, Meter Cb 2.1.

$$\bar{}\breve{}\bar{}\bar{}|\bar{}|\bar{}\bar{}\breve{}\breve{}\breve{}\bar{}\bar{}|\bar{}\bar{}$$

ad patr(em) ib(o) ut matris iram :: sib(i) esse sedatam sciat

962 **sibi**: dative of reference (AG 376); iambic shortening of *esse*.
sedatam < *sedo*, "appease, calm down."

963 **iam**: "soon." Eutychus is talking to those within the house.

964 **optuma opportunitate**: ablative of time or circumstance (AG 423).
ambo: "both of you."

965 **placida**: "friendly." Scan the second foot as a proceleusmatic, *tĭbĭ plăcĭd(a)*.
placata < *placo*, "calm."
cette: "give"; archaic imperative second person plural (see on 149).
nunciam: "immediately; at once."

966 **tibi**: Eutychus announces the bad news to Demipho.

967 **di te perdant**: "may the gods destroy you!"

968 **quin tibi ambo operam damus**: "in fact both of us pay attention to you."

969	Eutychus distinguishes between *genus*, one's family (including the ancestors), and *ingenium*, one's predisposed qualities from nature, inborn talent (or the opposite).
970	**degeneres**: "unworthy, ignoble, degenerate."
	inprobant < *inprobo*, "reject."
971	**tibi ergo**: iambic shortening of *ergo* (emphasis on *tib(i)*).
	eo: "therefore"; iambic shortening of *illud*.
973	**adulescenti amanti**: in apposition to *filio tuo*; dative of separation.
974	**ut**: "how" (exclamatory).
	dissimulat < *dissimulo*, "pretend."
976	**nouos amator, uetu' puer**: Notice the antithesis between the nouns and the adjectives (*nouus*= new, late). Eutychus makes fun of Demipho's love affair, coming so late in his life!
977	**perge**: See on 618.
	adsistam: "I shall stand by." Scan with hiatus after *perge* and prosodic hiatus after *ego*: *pērgĕ ĕgŏ ădsīst(am)*.
	hinc alterinsecus: "on this other side."
978	**quibus uerbis**: ablative of specification with *dignus* (AG 418b).
	oneremus < *onero*, "overwhelm."
981	**larua**: "insane" (always trisyllabic in Plautus). *laruae* were spirits of the dead that could appear throughout the year and torment the living by causing mental problems.
982	**temperare**: "to restrain, control"; + dative.
	istis ... artibus: i.e., Demipho's irrational love for Pasicompsa; *istis* is derogatory.
983	**deliqui** < *delinquo*, "misbehave."
984	**itidem ut tempus anni**: "just as the season of the year."
	aetate alia aliud factum conuenit: "one action is suitable at one time of life, another at another (time)," i.e., "different actions suit different seaons." *aetate* is an ablative of time; for the idiom with the repeated *alius* see AG 315c.
985	**senecta**: adjective modifying *aetate*.
	scortari (< *scortor*): "to associate with prostitutes"; in apposition with *istuc ius est*.
986	**ubi locist res summa nostra puplica**: "where are the affairs of our state going?" The illicit love affairs of old men disrupt

the function of the *res publica* and are therefore highly inappropriate; *loci*: partitive genitive.
ei: "alas."

987 **rei agendae isti**: "to conducting this business"; *rei*: i.e., falling in love. Scan with prosodic hiatus after *rei* (short syllable with synizesis) and with iambic shortening on *dare*.

988 **habete**: sc. *eam, puellam*.
cum porcis, cum fiscina: "lock, stock, and barrel." *porcis* < *porcus*, "pig"; *fiscina*: "basket," in which farmers used to put the refuse from the sows (*scrofae*) and their piglets. Demipho expresses indifference to Pasicompsa: "Take her and everything she is coming with!" According to the old man, everything happens in life for the best: Pasicompsa is metaphorically compared to a sow with pigs and therefore is not without faults (implied by the smelly *fiscina*); she is not worthy of his love after all.

989 **illi**: sc. *Charino*.
per me: "as far as I am concerned."
sibi habeat licet: "he is allowed to have her."

990 **temperi**: "at the right time" (locative of *tempus*).
non est copiae: "there is no opportunity."

991 **supplici sibi sumat quid uolt**: "let him exact whatever punishment he likes"; *quid= quidquid*.

992 **modo**= *dum modo*, "provided that"; proviso clause.

993 **adeo ioculo**: "just by way of a joke." The apodosis is in the imperfect subjunctive (*facerem*), whereas the protasis has pluperfect subjunctives (*sciuissem, dixisset*) in a mixed contrary-to-fact condition.

995 **subueni** < *subuenio*, "help"; present active imperative.

996 **hunc senem para clientem**: "make this old man your protégé."
memorem < *memor*, "mindful of"; + genitive.

997 **ignoscat** < *ignosco*, "forgive"; + dative.
delictis < *delictum*, "mistake."
adulescentiae: Lysimachus sarcastically calls Demipho's love for Pasicompsa a symptom of his rejuvation (see also Act II Scene ii).

998 **heia**: See on 950; scan *hēiā*.
superbe: "arrogantly."

inuehere= *inueheris* < *inuehor*, "attack."

999 **euenturum**: sc. *esse*, followed by a substantive result clause. Since Lysimachus would like to see Demipho fully punished, angry Demipho hopes that he can pay Lysimachus back one day.

parem: See 629; modifies *gratiam*.

1000 **missas ... istas artis feci**: "I have abandoned those ways of yours."

dehinc iam: "from now on."

1001 **consuetudine** < *consuetudo*, "habit."

1002 **loris** < *lorum*, "whip."

caedite < *caedo*, "beat, cut to pieces."

1003 **istuc**: "the thing you have just mentioned," i.e., whip him.

1004 **nihil opust resciscat**: "she does not need to find out."

quid istic: "well then, have it your way" (Enk 198).

1005 **eamus**: synizesis.

utibilest= *utibilis est*, "is appropriate."

1005-6 **factis tuis / ... arbitri ut sint qui praetereant per uias**: "so that the passers by will be judges for your deeds"; *praetereant* attracted into the subjunctive by *sint*. This is an allusion to the old Italic custom of folk-justice (*flagitatio* or *occentatio*) of accusing your debtor of injustice and insulting him in public.

1007 **eadem**: See 802.

fabula: "play." The joke breaks the dramatic illusion: the spectators are too tired and want to go home! Demipho will be further reprimanded inside the house.

1009 **illac**: "by that way."

hortum < *hortus*, "garden."

1010 **priu' ... quam**= *priusquam*; prosodic hiatus after *rem* and iambic shortening of *intro*.

1013 **uide**: "think."

mea fide: "on my word."

1015 **dicamus senibus legem**: "let us pass a law for old men."

1016 **qua se lege teneant contentique sint**: "by which law they should restrain themselves and be happy."

1017 **gnatus**= *natus*. The future tense, especially future imperative (see *prohibeto* in 1021), is common in the formulation of laws in Latin; *annos sexaginta*: see on 524.

1017 **si quem**= *si aliquem*.
scibimus= *sciemus*; introduces indirect statement: *quem ... scortarier* (1018).
1018 **caelibem** (< *caelebs*): "bachelor."
1019 **cum eo nos hic lege agemus**: "we will hereby deal with him under this law"; prosodic hiatus after *cum*.
inscitum (< *inscitus*): "stupid."
1020 **per nos**: cf. *per me* in 989.
egebit qui suom prodegerit: "he who squanders his money, will be in great need." *egebit* < *egeo*, "be in need"; *prodegerit* < *prodigo*, "squander."
1022 **quin amet et scortum ducat**: "from falling in love and having a mistress"; *quin* introduces clauses of prohibition after such verbs as *prohibeo* and a negative particle (*neu*). See AG 558.
quod bono fiat modo: "as long as it shall be done in a proper manner."
1023 **siquis prohibuerit, plus perdet clam <qua>si praehibuerit palam**: "if someone prevents (his son), privately he will lose more than (i.e., what he would lose) if he provided (the funds) openly *praehibuerit* < *praehibeo*, "provide"; *quasi* is used for conditional comparison, where the future-more-vivid comparison corresponds to a present contrary-to-fact condition in English.
1024 **haec adeo uti ex hac nocte primum lex teneat senes**: "may this law now from this night on for the first time apply to old men." *uti*= *ut*; prosodic hiatus on the second syllable of *uti* (iambic word).
1026 **senum**: genitive plural of *senex*.
clare plaudere: "to applaud noisily."